Through Life's Lens

Through Life's Lens

◆

A Memoir

Fred Bauman

iUniverse, Inc.
New York Lincoln Shanghai

Through Life's Lens
A Memoir

iUniverse books may be ordered through booksellers or by contacting:

iUniverse
2021 Pine Lake Road, Suite 100
Lincoln, NE 68512
www.iuniverse.com
1-800-Authors (1-800-288-4677)

ISBN-13: 978-0-595-41770-4 (pbk)
ISBN-13: 978-0-595-86113-2 (ebk)
ISBN-10: 0-595-41770-1 (pbk)
ISBN-10: 0-595-86113-X (ebk)

Printed in the United States of America

Dedicated to the memory of Vivian Bauman

Contents

Foreword

A memoir, by its very nature, is a recollection of people and events from a single point of view, one's own. But memory is selective, and after a while the mind plays tricks. Often when I relate a story to friends in the presence of my wife or children, I will hear "that's not the way I remember it," and I am sure it is not.

In this narrative I have tried to be as accurate about dates, names and events as possible. Of course I have been selective in my choices. A life of eighty some odd years can't be boiled down into chronological snapshots.

I may have embellished a little here and there for the sake of readability, but I think I have been honest about my feelings and tried to spare others embarrassment. With any kind of luck the final joke, hopefully, is on me.

1

The only reason I am alive today is because I could run faster than my best friend Helmut.

The year was 1936, the city Berlin. It was a time when killing Jews was a blood sport in Nazi Germany. They did not award any Olympic medals for it, but the new national anthem, the *Horst Wessel* song (named after a phony Hitler Youth martyr) did have lyrics that included, roughly translated, the exhortation to let the Jew's blood drip from your dagger. It was a time when the stridently anti-Semite propaganda organ of the Nazi party, *Der Stuermer*, equated Jews with vermin, to be exterminated.

They didn't stab Helmut, they hanged him on a lamp post. Those clean-cut Hitler Youths, wearing black shorts and brown shirts—in America they might have been Boy Scouts—chased Helmut and me as we were walking home from the private Jewish school we were forced to attend. Jews were no longer permitted in German public schools. There were four of them, none older than fifteen years, the pride of Hitler's Aryan Master Race. We were barely eleven.

"Filthy Jews!" they yelled at us as we tried to run. Helmut stumbled and fell as the quartet pounced.

To my everlasting shame I ran. I ran faster than I could ever have imagined. Better a live coward than a dead hero? Then why the recurring nightmares of that incident to this day? For a long while I blocked it out. Not until my mother mentioned the murder many years later did I finally let it back into my consciousness.

My mother was an only child, born in Pyritz, a small German town near the Polish border where my Omi (grandmother) owned a haberdashery store. She was in her thirties when she had her.

My father was the youngest of thirteen who vowed never to marry a woman with siblings. Enough relatives already, he used to say.

My parents actually were second cousins. The reason for that requires a rather lengthy explanation. So here goes.

We came by our surname of Baumann not through any long line of male ancestors, but through the kindness of a rabbi in a German-Polish border village. Sometime in the 1840s my father's grandmother fled the Russian Czar with four young sons, fearing their conscription into the army. Her husband either had died or been killed by Cossacks in one of many pogroms. All we know about his name is that people called him Bass, probably because of his deep voice. He was a cantor in a synagogue.

When his widow arrived in Germany, having bribed the border guards with the last of her money, the government had recently decreed that all citizens need identity papers. According to family gossip, the local rabbi took a shine to her and gave each son documents from a deceased member of his congregation. Obviously they must have been quite crude. Unfortunately they all bore different names. Thus one brother became a Jacobi, one a Heimann, one a Woolf and one, my grandfather, a Baumann. OK, so I spell my name with one 'n'. I used to tell people that when I immigrated to America I couldn't afford the other 'n' so I dropped it.

Brother Jacobi was the eldest. He grew up, married, and had a daughter, Sophie. Brother Baumann, the youngest, and Sophie's uncle, married twice. His first wife died in childbirth, so he married her sister, with whom he was actually in love. By Jewish custom he had to marry the older sister first. I am sure it was an arranged marriage. The girls came from the Boschwitz family. Rudy, one of their grand nephews, became a U.S. Senator from Minnesota.

Friedman Baumann's two marriages produced thirteen children. My father Caesar was the youngest of that brood. Thus his cousin Sophie was a whole generation ahead of him. When Sophie had her daughter Regi, my father was just five years older than the woman he would eventually marry, despite the fact that she was his second cousin. Ain't love grand. End of that story!

All I remember of my early years in Berlin is that we lived in large apartments where I could roller-skate in the corridors. I was an only son with an older sister who must have been very jealous of the way I was spoiled. My parents tried not to be preferential, but in those days the boy in a Jewish family got most of the attention. When the two of us misbehaved, the *ohrfeige* (a quick slap to the cheek) was always delivered first to my sister. I usually managed to run from my mother, dodging around furniture, until she began to laugh. It is pretty hard to mete out punishment while laughing.

Our family was well off, if not wealthy. My father was in the wholesale leather business, with ties to several large leather factories. We had a nanny, a chauffeur, a maid, and a cook, although cooks did not last long. My Omi, who lived with us, spent most of her time in the kitchen, telling the cook what to do. That had the predictable result.

Omi was a tiny woman with tremendous energy. She gave up her little store in Pyritz after her husband died and came to Berlin. At first my dad put her into a small apartment one floor above us, but she spent so much time in our flat that he soon felt it a waste of money.

One day while shopping on Berlin's main boulevard, the Kurfurstendamm, Omi was hit by a trolley car. It wasn't a life threatening injury, so instead of being taken to a hospital, she was brought home by the paramedics. In those days doctors made house calls. Our family physician, after patching up her scrapes and bruises, prescribed bed rest and no visitors for a week. I was about six years old and it seemed like a lifetime.

Finally I was allowed to see her. The curtains were drawn and the darkened room smelled of iodine. She looked so vulnerable. As I neared her bed she opened her eyes and tried to smile.

"Omi, I asked, are you dying?"

"No my sweet boy, I am not," she said.

"But tell me Omi," I whispered, "if you are, where do you keep your money?"

At that, Omi broke into loud laughter, causing my mother to rush in. When Omi told the story later to friends she insisted that I had shortened her convalescence period by days.

My grandma died at age 81, fixing sandwiches for the family in our London kitchen. The doctor said she had a massive heart attack and was dead before she hit the floor.

2

I think I loved my Omi more than any other member of the family. I spent many hours, literally hanging onto her apron strings, watching her cook. To this day I can make the best meatloaf, bake a delicious Gugelhupf or fix a gourmet dish of red cabbage with apples and raisins. Had World War II not interfered, I might have gone to hotel school in Geneva and become a chef.

I actually did spend a couple of years in Switzerland, at a private school in St. Moritz.

Helmut's murder was the catalyst for that turn of events. My parents wanted to get me out of harms way as quickly as possible. Although exit visas were required of anyone leaving the country and hard to come by, my father persuaded a friendly doctor to say that I suffered from tuberculosis and had to go to a sanitarium. It was a ruse to get me out of the country and it worked. I was eleven years old, and from that time on I spent more time away from my family than with them.

What I remember most about Belmunt, my Swiss school, is how I learned to ski, skate and play ice hockey. Poor little me, there I was, all alone in a foreign country with such a tough curriculum. I did however also have classes in Latin, math, history, composition and geography.

To get to St. Moritz from Berlin, one first has to take the express train to Zurich, have your carriage connected to the train for Chur and then change to a small gauge railroad up the mountain to your final destination. Beyond St. Moritz the train makes a couple more stops then turns around and comes back. Arriving in Chur I was met by a Belmunt staffer who made sure I would make the connection. We got off in St. Moritz, collected my luggage and were about to enter the van to the school when I discovered that I had left my teddy bear on the train. Yes, I was eleven, but a traumatized eleven, not knowing if I would ever see my family again. My teddy bear was my one connection to the past.

I threw a fit. When the stationmaster told me the train would return in an hour I refused to budge from the platform. No amount of cajoling could make me change my mind. My stubbornness was rewarded when, an hour later, my two-foot tall teddy returned, sitting in the window seat of an empty compartment, waiting to be reunited with his owner.

My teddy and I spent close to two years at Belmunt. Upon my departure I donated the fuzzy toy for the younger students to play with.

I don't know how my father managed to pay the tuition at this expensive institution. Getting money out of Germany was next to impossible unless it was smuggled out. My fellow students were an international melange, sons of diplomats, industrialists, financiers, educators and artists. Years later I discovered that the infamous Klaus von Bulow was one of them.

Every afternoon, summer or winter, we had to take a rest period on the veranda chaise lounges. Of course in cold weather we were bundled up. But even after it snowed, on most days the sun would send warm rays through puffy clouds.

Switzerland is a trilingual country where German, French and Italian is spoken, depending on where one lived. The maids who cleaned our rooms were mostly Italian. They used to get very upset when we traipsed in the wet slush from outside without first taking off our boots. One in particular invariably let off with a string of expletives that have stuck in my mind ever since. I have forgotten all the Italian I ever knew except those words: Imbecile, porco miserable, macaco, cretin, bambino stupido! Then she tried to take a swipe at us with her broom.

Sometime toward the end of my stay in Switzerland, my parents managed to get my sister Lili and my grandmother to a relative in Budapest. Then, in September of 1937 they themselves escaped the Nazis.

They should have left sooner.

My father was a decorated World War I veteran, having earned the Iron Cross fighting on the Western front. He was shot and seriously wounded in the groin by a French Colonial Goumier.

"He was wearing a red fez and I had him in my sights and could have shot him first while still in my trench," my father explained. "I just didn't want to kill anybody. But then the order came to go over the top and he got me instead."

As an Iron Cross recipient, my dad felt he was safe from the Nazis even after many of his friends and relatives were carted off to concentration camps. It could have been a fatal misconception. My parents were lucky to get out when they did.

One Sunday morning I got a phone call from my mother. She was crying, but they were tears of joy. We would all meet in Basel the next Wednesday and take a plane to London.

None of us had ever flown before. Thank God for barf bags. The mild turbulence outside was nothing compared to the inner turbulence of such an emotional reunion. We all got airsick, except for my Omi. This great lady, who was born before the invention of the automobile, let alone the airplane, took it all in stride. She actually enjoyed the ride and pronounced air travel the preferred method of transportation for now and future travel. She couldn't have known that a decade later I would fly out of her life on TWA Flight 3 to America, never to see her again.

When we arrived at Croydon, London's international airport at the time (Heathrow wasn't built until years later) we were met by my cousin Eri. His mother Martha, one of my father's sisters, had married an Englishman and was now running a boarding house in Brighton on England's south coast. Once rooms became available we were invited to stay there for a while, but our first few weeks in this new country were spent in one rented room in the Belsize Park section of London. It was there that cousin Eri drove us in his 1932 Austin 7 Ruby, a car built to seat four comfortably, but the six of us were a bit much. My sister sat on Dads lap in front and I squeezed between mother and Omi in the rear. Our luggage was left with customs to be picked up the following day.

The rented room had two double beds and a cot. Guess who would sleep on the cot? When we arrived there my grandmother did a strange thing. She peeled off the heavy karakul fur coat she had worn on the trip and asked my mother for a pair of small scissors mom kept in her purse. Then she sat down on the cot and cut off the coats three large buttons. They looked like fur covered hockey pucks.

"What on earth are you doing?" my mother asked speaking German of course.

Omi put a finger to her lips: "Sshhh, don't say anything, someone might hear!"

"Darling, were in England now, were safe!"

"You never know," my grandmother said as she pulled the fur from the first button. Left in her small, delicate hand was a large gold piece. She followed the routine with the other two buttons.

"I've had these since the war," Omi explained to my bewildered parents. "When the Kaiser asked everybody to give up their gold for the war effort, I wasn't about to. I melted down all the gold we had. This is it. I thought it might come in handy some day."

Dad came over to the cot and gave my Omi a huge hug. "Bless you, Sophie, you took a terrible risk. If the border guards had caught you they would have shot you on the spot." He had tears in his eyes.

That gold kept us in food and shelter for some time.

I only spent a couple of weeks with my parents. Obviously I had to go back to school. But not knowing one word of English presented a problem. Luckily there was a boarding school in Putney for cases such as mine. All teachers were bilingual, and although we were encouraged to learn and speak the new language as quickly as possible, we were allowed to communicate in German when absolutely necessary.

My sister and I both were enrolled in this school, an institution founded on the Montessori system. In that system the student does just about what he pleases as long as he does no harm. He can attend classes or not, take what subjects he chooses and learn at his own level.

For the first three months parents were not allowed to visit.

When my mother was permitted to finally look in on her children, she was first ushered into one of my sister's classes. There she was assured that her daughter was doing just great, quickly learning English and excelling in all subjects.

Then she asked to see me. "What classes is Fritzchen in?"

"Fritz is not attending any classes right now," he told her. He pointed to a large oak in the schoolyard. "He is climbing that tree."

My mother looked shocked.

"Let me assure you, Mrs. Baumann," he tried to persuade her, "when he is ready to learn he will come down from that tree and attend class."

"You don't know my Fritz," mother assured him, "He will never come down from that tree except to eat and sleep."

I was pulled out of that school faster than you can say Montessori System, and enrolled in a prep school for boys my age getting ready for high school. Amazingly enough I had picked up enough English during those three months to get by. It wasn't long before I spoke the language fluently.

Meanwhile my father was successful in establishing a new leather business. While it was still possible to travel in and out of Germany during the mid-thirties he had made many contacts and even opened a small branch office in London. That served him well after we emigrated.

In less than a year we were able to buy our own home in Hampstead Garden Suburb, one of London's newer housing developments. It was a two-story, four-bedroom, two and a half baths haven. We bought it while it was still under construction and watched it go up brick by brick. The type of mortgage dad insisted on had a clause that guaranteed payment in full should anything happen to him. That proved to be prescient.

My high school years were uneventful, except for the outbreak of World War II. The institution I attended was called Haberdashers Aske's Hampstead School, which is quite a mouthful. It was a public school, which means the parents, not the state paid for your tuition. Haberdashers constituted one of the great city guilds like Brewers, Drapers, Merchant Taylors and Goldsmiths of the 18th century which founded renowned public schools.

Early in 1940, when the London Blitz began for real, I was evacuated to the country. A year later I graduated, though not with honors or even a certificate of matriculation which would have enabled me to go to college. I enjoyed sports, in particular boxing and football. I played goalie for our second string in my senior year. Scholastically I barely scraped by with a GSC, a general school certificate, which merely stated that I had completed four years of higher education. I was not a good student. What I was, however, was a late bloomer. I did eventually attend college in America and graduated with a Bachelors degree in journalism.

3

Before my mother got married she studied the piano with hopes of becoming a concert pianist. She was well on her way, having performed successfully for local audiences, when marriage got in the way. According to her she never regretted giving up a musical career. She did, however, encourage me to follow in her footsteps. There were two pianos in our Berlin flat. A magnificent grand piano took up most of the space in our salon. An upright stood against the wall in an adjoining room. I began my piano lessons when I was seven.

It was my misfortune to be musically gifted. Supposedly I had perfect pitch, which is to say I could tell what note you were playing without looking. Reading music, at least the first few simple compositions, was a snap. Once I heard a piece I could play it by ear. That was my downfall. I paid scant attention to the written notes and played the piece my way. The easy way! The wrong way! I drove my piano teacher crazy.

"That's not the way it is written!" he would yell at me, rapping my knuckles with a ruler, "Look at the music! Play the notes on the page."

The final straw came when I spotted an accordion in the window of a music store while walking along the Ku-damm with my dad. It was a small, 8-bass Hohner.

"Buy me that accordion," I begged.

"Come on Fritz, you don't know how to play it," he countered.

"If I can play a whole song without a single mistake, bass chords and all, will you buy it?"

My dad felt he was on pretty safe ground. "You got a deal," he said.

Accordions have piano type keyboards for the right hand, albeit not as many octaves depending on their size, but played the same way. The left hand pushes

11

buttons to play bass notes and chords. One button, three or more notes. Easier really than the left hand on the piano.

We walked into that store and asked a salesman to show us the instrument displayed in the window. We walked out of that store with me owning it. Haven't I already said that I was spoiled?

When my piano teacher found out he refused to give me further lessons. "That's an instrument of the devil," he complained. "Fritz will lose all sense of touch and tone. Either it goes or I go."

Guess who went?

It didn't take many years for me to graduate first to a 48-bass and finally to a 120-bass Hohner, with triple couplers for the right hand. While still in my teens I formed a six-piece combo with a group of friends. We were welcomed at weddings, bar mitzvahs and local club dances.

Strange how things turn out sometimes. My saxophone player, doubling on clarinet went by the name of Stitch. He had us in stitches most the time. His real name was Gerard Hoffnung. He would arrive for practice on his bicycle, one trouser pant tucked into his knee-length hose, different in color from the other one, a stocking cap streaming in the wind behind him, his saxophone case strapped over one shoulder. He became a famous cartoonist for Punch Magazine and leader of an orchestra featuring strange instruments such as vacuum cleaner hoses, and a timpanist with his nose heavily bandaged. Unfortunately Stitch died at an early age.

I think my mother regretted letting me have my way. I never became the piano virtuoso she might have enjoyed listening to vicariously. When I quit piano lessons I was studying Nola, a piece written in the key of D. Unfortunately I never got out of that key. To this day, when I play the piano, I transpose every song into D-major.

My father was fond of telling me that I could become anything I wanted to as long as it was a leather merchant. He was serious.

Soon after graduating from high school I was apprenticed to G.W. Russell & Sons, a leather factory in Hitchin, Hertfordshire, about an hours train ride north of London. Once again I was alone in a strange town away from my family. My parents paid for my room and board in a private residence not far from work. I was sixteen at the time.

The manufacture of leather is a fairly complicated procedure, especially for fine leathers such as suede. It all starts with hides from cows, sheep and other ruminants, the first step involving a soaking of the hides in cold water mixed with detergents, salts and biocides. Next the hair has to be removed by another soaking process called liming which involves various other chemicals. In my father's day, believe it or not, dog manure was used, because it contained essential enzymes. The chemicals used by Russell &Sons stank just as bad. Their yard was huge. Transporting bales of hides undergoing the various stages of tanning and dyeing required a small truck, or lorry, as it was called in England. That's where I came in. I became the schlepper though I'm sure my employers had never heard that term.

My job was to load the lorry at one building in their block-long yard and unload it at another, a half block away. One of the destinations was the dye loft. Its entrance was up an outside wooden staircase. Some of those bales weighed a ton. Over one hundred pounds at times. Lawrence the lorry driver helped load them onto my back, leaving me to climb those stairs. It was tiring work, but I was young and strong.

One day I asked Lawrence if he would teach me how to drive.

I never knew whether Lawrence was his first or last name. Protocol in English commerce was to address superiors by their last names, preceded by a Mr. Mrs. or Miss. At G.W. Russell it was different. Since the three brothers running the factory all were Russell's, it was Mr. George, Mr. Harry, or Mr. Sam.

After I bugged him for a week, Lawrence finally gave in and began teaching me the basics. Starting, stopping or steering was a cinch, but changing gears was another matter. You had to double de-clutch every time to avoid grinding the gears or, worse still, strip them. Nevertheless, after a couple of month I had it down pat. I actually drove the lorry several times, earning Lawrence's approval. Naturally, I was not permitted outside the yard.

One day, while backing up to the dye loft staircase, my foot slipped off the brake pedal and I smashed into the wooden structure. The crash broke the first three steps and part of the railing. I was sure I would get canned on the spot. But I wasn't. I found out later that not only was my father subsidizing my wages but he also paid for the damages.

Often after work I would stroll down to the Red Lion, a cozy little pub just down the street from the tannery, for a shandy. A shandy consists of half beer half lemonade, with very little alcohol content. At my age anything stronger probably would not have agreed with me.

One evening I was standing at the bar, waiting for my drink, when three American airmen staggered through the door, obviously under the influence. It was the first time that I had ever met any Americans. The U.S. Eighth Air Force had recently arrived in England and was establishing air bases to help fight the war against the Axis.

The three Yankees made it up to the bar and ordered beer. Suddenly, without any warning, the airman next to me turned and spat out a wad of chewing tobacco. It landed on my left foot.

"I say old chap," I complained in my best Oxford English accent, "you really can't do that sort of thing over here!"

With that the airman pulled a vicious looking knife from his belt and scratched a deep groove along the top of the bar.

"Listen, limey," he drawled, "I'm a hunnert percent 'merican, and I can fucking spit where I want to. If you don't like it," he slurred his words a little and pointed the knife at my belly, "how would you like me to s-s-stick this right here?"

It was a moment in my life I shall never forget. For some strange reason I did not feel afraid, I felt angry, but not scared. In my high school one of the mandatory Phys-Ed classes had been boxing, and I was pretty good at it. Calling on my knowledge of the sport, I quickly sidestepped the knife and let loose with a powerful punch straight for the guy's nose. I made sure to put all my body power behind it.

My adversary dropped to the floor, blood streaming from his nose.

Now his buddies are going to kill me, I thought.

But they didn't. Instead they picked up their fallen comrade and dragged him out the door. To say I was surprised would be an understatement, until I happened to look behind me.

There, standing side by side, with arms folded across their chests were five British Rangers, an elite fighting force of warriors, none of them under six feet. I don't know why I hadn't noticed them before. They just stood there, not saying a word, winking at me and smiling. Had it come to a brawl the Yankees wouldn't have stood a chance, especially in their condition.

I offered to buy a round of drinks but my new friends refused.

"No thanks, mate," one of them wearing sergeant major stripes said. "We think you handled that bloody well. Our pleasure."

That's when it hit home. My knees felt weak and I had to sit down. As the rangers left I said a silent prayer for their future safety. Then finally, I drank my shandy.

There is an aftermath to the story.

While I was sitting at a table toward the back of the pub trying to get my strength back, the entrance door swung open, and in walked the very airman I had knocked down. He looked around the room with bloodshot eyes until they focused on me.

Before I had a chance to escape, he staggered over to my table and said: "Shay fellow, doan I know you? Lemme buy you a drink." I politely declined and got out of there.

I'm willing to bet that groove is still there today, atop the Red Lions bar, a bar that had seen better than a century of service. Things don't change much in the British Isles.

4

It was in Hitchin that I fell in love for the first time. The object of my affection was Colleen, a Land Army girl.

As men left the farms to enlist in the military, women were recruited to take their place. An organization called the LAC, or Land Army Corps, was formed by the British government consisting of volunteers age sixteen to twenty-five, all strapping young girls who could drive tractors, plow the land or pitch hay with the best of them. They wore smart uniforms, khaki jodhpurs, green woolen sweaters and Canadian Mounties style hats with the large hard brims and pointed tops.

Colleen was one of the prettiest girls I ever met. Her Irish heritage showed in her green eyes, rosy cheeks and upturned nose. Her wavy hair was auburn, cut regulation short. They didn't want the girls' hair caught in any machinery.

We met because she had a flat tire on her bicycle. Her misfortune was my good luck. I carried a small repair kit and tire pump on my Raleigh three-speed and just happened to pass by at the right moment. She accepted my offer of help. After I had patched her inner tube and pumped the tire back up I introduced myself. She told me her name was Colleen Connelly.

"My friends call me Cee-Cee," she said.

Her name had an Irish lilt to it and not just because of the alliteration. It was music to my ears.

Cee-Cee thanked me and asked how she could reciprocate my kindness.

Silly girl!

"How about going on a date with me?" I suggested. She gave me a funny look as my heart pounded in my chest.

"I don't know anything about you except that you are a true gentleman, at least as far as fixing flats goes." She smiled. "Are you from here?"

"For now I am. I work at the tannery. But my home is in London. So what is it you want to know about me?"

"Tell you what," Colleen suggested. "How about you and I going out for fish and chips Saturday night? But we'll go Dutch."

"Sounds marvelous. What time and where shall we meet? Do you know where the Red Lion is? Perhaps we can have a drink there first. How does six o'clock sound?"

"That's good. But I have to go milk the cows now. I only came to town to get some stamps." She held out her hand for me to shake. "Too-dle-oo."

As I watched her ride out of sight I knew I was in love.

We did not get to a kissing stage for several weeks after that first date. When we went to the cinema she let me put my arm around her but when my other hand strayed toward forbidden territory she gently but firmly placed it back in my lap.

Then came the night of the picnic.

At the outskirts of Hitchin there is a grass and shrub covered, gentle rise, known as North Hill. It is, at least it was then, the favorite spot for young lovers. Couples brought picnic baskets and blankets on balmy summer nights, and while the blankets served as table cloths during the meal, once the food was gone, one could often find the young man atop the young lady and the blanket atop both of them, serving as cover. Sex in public areas, as long as it was done discreetly, was tolerated in England in those days. After all, there was a war on, don't you know. Live for the day, tomorrow may be your last.

Colleen and I decided to have a North Hill picnic about one month into our relationship. She would bring the food and I the blanket and apple cider. Cider, was one of her favorite beverages. It had just enough of an alcohol content to get a kick from.

Our dates by that time were ending with a good night kiss but not much more. Relieving myself in bed afterwards was no substitute for the real thing. Thus I determined that North Hill should be my solution.

We finished the cold chicken, potato salad, and brownies Colleen had baked, and were cleaning up our mess. I took the paper plates and wrappings to a garbage bin on the grounds and returned to our spot. Colleen had wiped her lips and was applying some lipstick.

"I didn't know you used lipstick," I said, "I always thought your beautiful complexion was natural."

"My poor naive little Freddy," she said, "every girl puts on a little lipstick, but that's the only makeup I use."

"Is it kiss proof?" I asked

"Why don't you try it?" she teased

I put my arms around her and gently maneuvered us down onto the blanket. Dusk had settled in and a full moon was beginning to rise in the east.

"I think I'm in love with you," I panted after a prolonged smooch that topped anything we had done before. "I want to make love to you."

I put my hand on her crotch and this time she did not pull it away.

"I want you too, sweetheart," she whispered, as she felt my erection, "but I can't."

"So tell me why not?" I asked, slightly frustrated.

"It's the wrong time of the month," she explained. She guided my hand between her legs. "There," she said, "can you feel the pad?"

That night there was no need for me to take myself in hand. I experienced spontaneous relief when Colleen placed my hand on her crotch. It messed up my underwear, I but now I had something to look forward to. Or so I thought.

On our next date a week later she was still menstruating, as she did a week after that and the week following. What did I know? My sweet Colleen evidently had a medical problem. That poor girl had a menstrual cycle that saw her on the rag six months at a stretch. Meanwhile my right hand was working overtime.

My mother and I had always been open about the facts of life. I knew where babies came from and how they were made from the age of eight. I was however confused then about the exact biological makeup of a woman's reproductive system. I thought the penis had to be inserted into the rectum. That thought disgusted me and I declared firmly that I would never engage in that sort of activity. Yeah, right!

I spoke with my mother about Colleen's problem on one of my rare visits to London. Travel was restricted during the war. The troops needed most available space and civilians were discouraged from using the railroads.

Mother had a hard time trying not to laugh me out of the room.

"No girl has a period lasting longer than a week," she said."Your young lady would be making medical history. She'd more likely be in the Guinness Book of Records. No, no, no, Freddylein, (sometimes my mother would add the German diminutive syllable to my English name) that girl has no intention of having sex with you. She is using her sanitary napkin as a protective device in more ways than one!"

My mother chortled. "I am not making fun of you," she insisted. "Sorry, but this whole situation strikes me as very funny."

My buddy Lawrence at the plant put it more succinctly.

"She's a bloody prick teaser, that one is," he said. "You'd have no trouble getting into Elsie in the dye loft. Elsie thinks you're good looking enough to be in the movies."

Lawrence was talking about the crew chief for a half dozen girls who were scrubbing dyes onto skivers. They wore long aprons and large rubber gloves as they dipped brushes into buckets of dye. The liquid was splashed on skins stretched out on stone slabs. These were tilted away from the dyer, allowing surplus dye to run back into troths, from where it drained back into a bucket.

Skivers are split parts of the cowhide, used for cheaper leather goods such as wallets or purses. Once dyed, the skins are embossed with imitation grains, making them look like the real thing. Sometimes 'genuine' alligator or snake skin leather is nothing more than an embossed skiver.

Elsie was a funny but foul-mouthed original, somewhat chubby, who thought nothing of grabbing my crotch and teasing me about still being a virgin.

"You bloody well ought to be in Hollywood," she insisted, "you're better looking than most them matinee idols. Why waste your time in this fucking place?"

Elsie was old enough to be my mother and I was genuinely fond of her. But to break my maiden, for wont of a better phrase, I would have had to be drunk and blind. I also think she didn't bathe more than once a week, if that often.

5

As my apprenticeship continued at the Russell yard I was assigned to a different department every few months so I could learn the business from the ground up. I was well on the way to follow in my fathers footsteps when one morning, a few months from my eighteenth birthday, I was called into Mr. George's office. The oldest brother of the Russell clan, he always reminded me of a Falstaff like character, the jovial fat knight in a Shakespeare play. He had a bristling, white mustache, rosy cheeks and a perpetual smile.

This morning he was not smiling.

"I am sorry my boy," he said, "but you are wanted in London. I just got a phone call, and it appears your father is very sick. You had better leave right away. I'll inform everyone that you will be gone for a few days." He took me by the arm, patted me on the back and steered me out of his office.

The journey from Hitchin to London normally takes an hour. On this trip my train got shunted to a sidetrack several times to let troop trains pass. We finally made it to Kings Cross station from where I could catch a bus to my house.

I had not taken the time to call home so I knew nothing of my dad's condition. I knew it had to be serious or Mr. George would not have sent me home. As I stepped off the Number 2 bus on Lyttleton Road, about five blocks from our house, a neighbor lady was about to get on. When she saw me she gave me a hug and said: "Oh you poor boy, you poor, poor boy." Then she boarded the bus.

"Why am I a poor boy?" I asked, as the bus took off with her standing on the rear platform.

"Oh dear, you don't know, do you? I'm so sorry, I should never have…."

The rest of her sentence was lost to engine noise as the bus accelerated, and she stepped inside to find a seat on the Double Decker.

Walking home as fast as I could, I knew I had come too late. My father was dead. The neighbor's words assured me of that.

My sister and grandmother met me at the door. Both were crying.

"It happened during the night," my sister sobbed. "We called Doctor Levi but he couldn't save him. Mom's upstairs. The doctor gave her a shot."

I saw my father for the last time, a cold, stiff corpse, stretched out on his bed under a sheet. A napkin was tied under his chin, knotted at the top of his head to keep his jaw from dropping open. A large silver coin covered each eye. My mother sat next to him on the bed, rocking back and forth, obviously in shock. Whatever the doctor gave her didn't knock her out. I bent down over her and gave her a kiss. She stared at me, silently, for the longest time. Then she said:

"You're the man of the house now."

Before I could answer the undertaker showed up to remove the body.

Jewish tradition tries to assure a quick interment, usually within 48 hours from the time of death. Bodies are not embalmed and cremation is against religious belief. My father was placed into a simple wooden coffin and buried in London's Jewish cemetery in Willesden. Following a short ceremony and prayers, it was my duty to throw the first shovel of dirt on his coffin. The clods made a haunting, hollow sound I hoped I would never have to hear again.

Through the years, as traditions got more relaxed among some Jews, cremation became an option. My mother died and was cremated in 1971. She wanted her ashes to be buried next to my father in Willesden, but rabbinical protocol forbade it. I had visions of creeping into that cemetery in the middle of the night with a shovel and her urn. In the end what difference does it make in the greater scheme of things? Her memory is in my heart and mind, not some plot of earth. Eventually the rabbinate relented and now mother's ashes rest in a grave next to my father.

When I turned eighteen I tried to enlist in the Royal Air Force. I was a member of the Air Cadets, a sort of ROTC, meant to train future airmen in various skills.

Those ranged from folding parachutes, to engine mechanics, aerodynamics, spotting enemy planes, and eventually actual experience in flying gliders. Our squadron was number 1066. Since that was the year of William the Conqueror, in a very bad pun attempt, I called my jazz combo the '1066 Corncurers'. Yeah, like that would fly!

Imagine my surprise when our squadron commander told me I could no longer be a member of the group. The reason: I was classified as an enemy alien. Even though I was stateless, had been exiled from Germany because of my religion, and fully intended to become a British subject, I was a foreigner who could not serve his adopted country. The only one happy with that situation was my mother. She was relieved that now I would not be shot out of the skies by any Baron von Richthoven wannabe.

I would not give up however. I tried joining the army, navy, coastguard, or any other branch of the military that would have me. I appealed to the Home Secretary to no avail. I did get an official letter from that worthy, thanking me for my patriotism, and assuring me that should the rules change he would so inform me and enable me to enlist. He did suggest that I could aid the war effort by undergoing government training in some essential industry such as airplane manufacturing or the like.

That's what I did. After a three months government sponsored training period I became an apprentice tool and die maker in a company that made plastic parts for fighter plane radio gear. In America I would have been a male Rosie the Riveter.

Enlistment regulations for victims of Nazi persecution did eventually change. The British Military established the Pioneer Corps, a highfalutin' name for an outfit whose primary function was digging latrines. That was not for me.

For the next couple of years I lived at home, much to the delight of my mother and grandmother. That kind of situation is not conducive to a young man's love life however.

I was nineteen and still a virgin.

The war was dragging into its fifth year. Nazi bombs had almost destroyed London, Manchester, Coventry and other cities. Bombers were being replaced with Hitler's secret weapons. First came the V-1s, also called buzz bombs, because of their distinctive put-put sound meant to instill fear. The scary part came when the rocket engines quit and there was no more sound. You knew the missile had begun its dive to the ground somewhere close.

Following that weapon came the even scarier V-2, a faster than the speed of sound rocket that did tremendous damage on impact, but gave no warning sound on approach to its target. Once you heard the sonic boom you knew you were safe, this time anyway.

One night a V-2 hit about a block from our house, completely obliterating three large homes. It was an implosion more than an explosion that sucked out some of our front windows. The concussion threw me out of my bed and onto the floor. When my mother came bursting into the room I was lying there motionless, wrapped in my blankets, to all appearances dead. She knelt by my side and began to scream. That's when I woke up. I had slept, unhurt, through the whole thing. Talk about being a sound sleeper.

We had made it unscathed this far. Some of our friends were not so lucky.

6

Shortly after the beginning of hostilities, when the Nazis invaded Poland and threatened the rest of Europe, Karl Goeritz, my father's best friend, decided to leave Holland with his family. They had fled there earlier to escape Hitler. Karl, his wife Irmi and their two infant children booked passage for South America on the Simon Bolivar, one of the last passenger ships allowed to leave with refugees aboard.

On the morning of November 18, 1939, about an hour out of Rotterdam, the Simon Bolivar either hit a German mine or was hit by a torpedo from a U-Boat. Standing on the deck, Karl was enjoying the fresh salt air, his young wife and children by his side. They were celebrating their good fortune at having escaped the Nazis one more time.

The explosion hurled jagged chunks of metal through the air, one hitting Karl in the back, killing him instantly. As the ship began to capsize and sink, Irmi was thrown into the water but managed to hold on to her children. An excellent swimmer, she struggled to escape patches of burning oil and began treading water, hoping a lifeboat or other rescue vessel would pick her up. When none came she began to swim away from the sinking ship, holding one child under each arm, keeping their heads above water.

Hours passed. Irmi became more and more exhausted. Time came when she could no longer hold on to both babies. One slipped out her grasp. Still she swam on. But try as she might, she could not hold on to the second child. At that point Irmi decided life was not worth living. She surrendered herself to the waves.

That's all she remembered later. She thought she passed out. Evidently she kept on swimming by sheer instinctive reflex.

Irmi Goeritz was rescued by an English Coast Guard vessel and brought to Folkstone harbor along with other survivors. Eighty-four people drowned.

My father knew that the Goeritzes were sailing aboard the Simon Bolivar. Immediately upon hearing about the disaster he drove down to Folkstone where survivors were being taken. He found Irmi, wrapped in a Red Cross blanket, soaked in dirty oil, refusing cups of hot tea, almost catatonic, endlessly repeating the names of her two children.

"Everybody's dead," she moaned, rocking back and forth. "The babies are dead, Karl is dead. Why am I alive? Let me die, please, let me die."

My father waited so see if there were more survivors, hoping against hope that one of the babies or even Karl had been saved. That was not to be. He brought Irmi home to our house. My mother gave her a hot bath and put her to bed. Weeks would pass before Irmi got back up out of that bed.

At first Irmi refused to take any nourishment, but hunger eventually got the better of her. She had tea with toast the third day, then began to eat some food at mealtimes, when mother brought a tray to her bed. But she did not talk and refused to get up.

Three weeks passed by.

My sister and mother took turns feeding her. Nobody would actually say it, but Irmi's presence was beginning to become an inconvenience. Then, out of the blue, on Monday morning of the fourth week as I was passing by her open bedroom door, I thought I heard her call my name.

"Fritzchen, she called," not knowing people now called me Fred, "komm doch mal hierher." (Do come here).

I knocked on the door and entered, stepping gingerly. The curtains where drawn but she asked me to open them. It was the first time I heard her speak since her arrival.

"Please bring me a hairbrush and a mirror," she asked me in German. "I have decided to live!"

And live indeed she did.

Irmi eventually immigrated to America, where she met and married her second husband with whom she had two daughters.

By one of life's little coincidences I knew the man before she did. Dr. Henry Selver was the headmaster of 'PriWaKi', my Jewish school in Berlin.

I indulge in a little name dropping here. Two of my fellow students were Mike Nichols, although his name then was Michael Igor Peschowski, and former Secretary of the Treasury Michael Blumenthal. Although Dr. Selver did not become that famous, he had a successful career as a high-ranking administrator with UNICEF.

Despite that terrible tragedy and everything else she went through, Irmi Selver was a survivor and an inspiration to us all.

◆　　　◆　　　◆

While still living at home I did my best to keep up with the dating scene. After all, there were not that many available men my age left around. Most were serving with the armed forces. To be sure, Yanks on leave were highly desirable and great competition. They not only had money to burn, they could give the ladies coffee, chocolate and nylons.

If that wasn't bad enough, what girl wanted to sit around a dance floor all evening, waiting for the accordion player to get off the bandstand at midnight?

I was cautiously hopeful therefore, when a certain little bus conductress seemed to take a shine to me on my regular morning ride to work.

Bus conducting was another occupation filled by women while the men were at war.

Maureen was a redhead like Colleen, cute as a bug, and sassy in a charming sort of way when I flirted with her.

I was a few years older now and wiser to the ways of women, so a repeat of my North Hill experience was unlikely. But I had still not crossed the Rubicon in my march to nirvana. I know I'm mixing metaphors here, but what can I say? I just wanted to get laid.

I asked Maureen for a date and she said yes. Saturday night would be fine.

'Arsenic and Old Lace', starring Cary Grant, was showing at the Leicester Square Theater. We planned to meet outside the lobby around a quarter to eight. Maureen actually showed up on time as I was standing in line for our tickets. The movie was a very funny and we both enjoyed watching it. Since it was our first date I behaved like a true gentleman.

Do you know Cary Grant's real name? I asked as we exited the theater.

"Don't know as I do."

"Archibald Leach."

"You're kidding!"

"No, really, but can you imagine a marquee spelling out 'Starring Archibald Leach'? I asked. "Boris Karloff's real name is William Henry Pratt, and he was born in London."

We were holding hands and she stopped briefly to kiss me on the cheek.

"Thank you very much, I really enjoyed that," she said.

"The night is young, how about a nightcap?" I suggested. "Have you ever been to the Angel & Crown? It's a great old pub, right around the corner on St. Martins Lane."

"I'll go for a Gin and Orange," Maureen agreed, "but I mustn't miss the last bus."

"Don't worry about that sweetheart, you're with the last of the big spenders. I am taking you home in a taxi."

"Oh no, you mustn't!"

"Oh yes I must."

"Well, we'll see."

Maureen had two gins and orange while I nursed 'alf of a 'alf 'n 'alf,' half a pint of beer, half mild, half bitter. I really didn't care much for alcohol. She did not put up much of a struggle when I hailed a cab.

"Where to governor?" the cabby asked.

Maureen gave him her address. "But stop a few houses before you get there, I got a nosy landlady."

On the ride home we got into it pretty heavy. The cabdriver had to ask twice: "Is this all right?" as he stopped a short distance from Maureen's house.

I paid the cab fare and walked Maureen the rest of the way.

When we got to her house she put a finger to her lips and warned me to be quiet.

"My landlady doesn't allow male visitors," she whispered, "she'd kick me out for sure. But I know some of the girls have had boyfriends in."

She walked up the three steps to her front door.

"Take off your shoes and stay close to me. We have to sound like one person climbing the stairs."

I tiptoed up two flights to her room feeling conspiratorial. Once we were safely inside Maureen breathed a sigh of relief. Again she put a finger to her lips. I pulled her close to me and kissed her long and hard. I pointed to the bed.

"No!" She shook her head as she kept her voice low. "It creaks something awful. She is bound to hear us."

Maureen took a matchbox from a shelf to light a small gas fire. Soon it gave off a warm, orange glow. She tossed two large throw pillows on the rug and motioned me to lie down next to her. The only light in the room came from the fireplace.

Gently I reached under her skirt and began pulling down her panties. She helped me get rid of them and started to unbuckle my belt. In no time flat my pants and skivvies were down around my ankles. Becoming ever more aroused, I dared to feel the moistness between her legs. My sexual fantasies were about to bear fruition. I was ready to enter the tunnel of love.

All of a sudden I was struck with an irresistible urge to pee. It was about a strong as one could imagine.

"Where is the loo?" I whispered with undisguised urgency.

"It's a half flight down the stairs, but you can't use it. The old witch is bound to see you. You can't, really, you can't go." Maureen was adamant.

As in many of England's small hotels and rooming houses, the lavatory was a shared facility for the use of several guests, sometimes as many as three. If I couldn't use Maureen's loo, there was nothing left for me to do but to leave in a hurry. The only thing that kept me from soiling her carpet was the fact that it is almost impossible to urinate from an erect penis, especially one like mine, hard enough to drive nails.

I pulled up my pants, grabbed my shoes and rushed out of Maureen's rooming house as fast as I could without making too much noise. The moment I hit the street, I relieved myself against the nearest tree.

The great satisfaction from being able to heed nature's call was marred only by knowing that there was no way I could return to Maureen that night.

The buses and subway trains had long since stopped running. I had to walk home six miles from Maureen's flat to our house. It took the better part of two hours. And I had nothing to show for it.

A couple of days later I received a love note in my mail. It was from Maureen:

"Dearest Fred," it read, "I am so very sorry about last night. I really like you. I hope you feel as strongly as I do about resuming where we left off. Thanks again for everything but next time bring a potty. Love and xxx, Maureen."

There! That was the sass I loved so much about my little redhead. Of course I wanted to see her again, but fate intervened, fate in the form of an advertisement in the Evening Standard, London's most popular afternoon newspaper.

7

The American Army is looking for personnel who speak fluent German and possibly one other language to enlist in the newly formed Civil Censorship Division. All food, clothing and lodging provided. Good pay with opportunity for promotion. Must be willing to serve in Occupied Germany. Contact Captain Sperber at No. 40 Portman Place.

That ad had the effect on me of a red flag waved at a bull, except in a good way. I charged right over there the very next day, filled out an application and was accepted on the spot. Then I went home to tell my mother. Her reaction was predictable.

"I won't let you go," she declared. "I'll never sign a consent form. You've stayed out of the army all this time, I don't care whose army it is, you're not becoming a soldier now!"

"Mom, First of all I don't need your consent, I'm over eighteen now. Secondly I am not becoming a soldier, we will be civilians in uniform. It's a terrific opportunity. The pay is great, Ill send most of it home."

"I don't want your money." Tears started to well up as she resorted to her crying mode, "I don't want you to get killed."

"What killed, mom? The war is over, remember VE day? I'm not going to the Pacific."

"If only your father were alive! He'd never permit it."

There, the other shoe had dropped. Invoking my father's name. I can't leave her, I was the man of the house, what good Jewish son doesn't look after his widowed mother?

It all instilled that old Jewish guilt as intended, just not enough of it. I joined the American Army the next week. A new phase of my life was about to begin.

Other than calisthenics at six a.m., our basic training was nothing like army boot camp. We were a motley group of mostly young men and women from various countries, with German Jews in the majority. The Civil Censorship Division of the American 7th Army group came under the classification of G-2, army intelligence. Yeah, I know. That's supposed to be an oxymoron. But we took ourselves seriously, and we were taken seriously by our superiors at camp in the north of England.

We were training to become postal censors. That meant that every piece of mail coming from or going to Occupied Germany would face our scrutiny. What we were told to look for was microfilm or micro dots, the latter possibly hidden under postage stamps, and even coded messages, perhaps revealing hiding places of Nazi war criminals.

Other than rank insignia, our uniforms were identical to those of regular army GIs. We were classified ACEs, Allied Civilian Employees. Later, once we were stationed in Germany, we would be joined by our American counterparts, WDEs, War Department Employees. At first those made twice as much money and could wear officers' uniforms, but that changed eventually.

One of those WDEs and I became very close. Bedmates close, even though she was fourteen years my senior and married. Her name was Celia. She was a Brooklyn schoolteacher, but felt it her civic duty to work for the government during this reconstruction period begun by the Marshall Plan.

I'll return to Celia later.

My first duty station in Germany was Pullach, a suburb of Munich. Our headquarters were the underground bunkers once occupied by Martin Bormann, Hitler's deputy Fuehrer. These quarters may have been underground but they lacked nothing in comfort and luxury. Air-conditioned offices, furnished with plush leather chairs, mahogany desks, piped in music, we had it all. Here is an excerpt from a letter I wrote home to England in the fall of 1945.

I got promoted at work today. What we do is top secret so I can't really tell you much about it. Only ten of us have been chosen for this assignment. What I can say is that we deal with correspondence from people like von Ribbentrop, Krupp, Messerschmidt, you name it. It is a nice feeling that I am doing an important job. The German people are all peace loving and law abiding citizens. There never were any Nazis! They all hated Hitler and were forced to join the party, especially those who joined in 1933. Concentration camps were pure enemy propaganda. I get sick listening to them. Actually they are not far from starving and it serves them right. They are docile as sheep, smile at your face but cuss you out as soon as your back in turned. Every time I hear a hard luck story from a Kriegsverwundeter (wounded veteran) I say right to his face Das verdanken Sie Ihrem Fuehrer. (You have your Fuehrer to thank for that.).

We did not have to work weekends. A few weeks into my Munich stint I managed to take a trip to Berchtesgaden, after first visiting Mozart's birthplace in Salzburg, Austria. From there our group went up to the Berghof, Hitler's favorite residence. Imagine a group of German Jews tromping all over that once Holy Grail. I signed my name in large letters on a wall in the house, above which I scrawled 'A happy Jew'.

As satisfying as my work was, I jumped at the opportunity for an even more challenging task. Because of my erstwhile entertainment background,—I had packed my accordion and played it on occasion—I was transferred to Special Services.

My duties now changed drastically. I was assigned my own jeep and, since we did not carry any weapons, two armed guards if I deemed them necessary. I furnished and opened an Officers Club and drove around the area scouting musical groups and other local talent for gigs there. Eventually I was able to book some USO shows, though top talent performed only at larger venues.

In addition to the club, I started a biweekly divisional newspaper, arranged ski trips to the local mountains, commandeered fifty bicycles from a German factory for the use of our people and even managed to secure a stable of riding horses. I earned the respect of our commanding officer and the gratitude of our group. Only once did I almost get into big trouble.

Just about any furnishings for whatever enterprise we were running came from what was euphemistically called liberated German property. In charge of this confiscation practice was the American Military Government. Everything had to be done through channels, by the book, in triplicate. Only former Nazi party members were subject to confiscation procedures. Those, of course, were not hard to find.

When we moved our club to larger premises we needed more furniture. Asking the Military Government for the stuff required proper documentation, dutifully signed by the appropriate officers. As it happened, our C.O. was on leave. He was the only one qualified to okay the request I had drawn up. It included a lot, and I mean a LOT of furniture. We had heard of a warehouse in Frankfurt that was being besieged with similar requests, first come, first served. What else could I do? I forged the colonel's signature.

Herbie Steinberg, my partner in Special Services, and I drove two big army trucks to Frankfurt and loaded up. Then we drove to Military Government HQ and dropped the necessary documents on the desk of the major in charge.

While he was not in his office.

We should of course have done it the other way around. We were long gone when he returned, steaming mad, as we found out later. Our Col. Eggert got a call from the major when he returned from leave.

"Those two clowns cleaned us out!" the major stormed. "How could you okay such an enormous request, sir? Most of that stuff was supposed to go to General Patton's headquarters, sir."

"First of all you must be aware that General Patton is no longer military governor of Bavaria, major, too lenient to the Nazis, I hear. He's been made 15th Army commander. But I'm sure you knew that. So, what's all this crap about where the furniture was going? I am sure you can find replacements quite easily, major. Those boys did all right by our group. You must be sure and enjoy their hospitality if you're ever down our way."

The major really had very little response left. I guess rank has its privileges.

Following that conversation, Col. Eggert called us into his office to read us the riot act.

"Baumann, are you aware that you were authorized to sign my name as long as you signed yours in the appropriate spot?" he thundered at me. "Do you realize that if you were military instead of civilian I could have you court-martialed?"

"Yes sir, colonel, I'm sorry."

'Sorry doesn't hack it, Baumann, I am fining you a weeks pay. Are we clear? At ease!"

I had been standing stiffly at attention during the colonel's harangue. Now he got up and came around to the front of his desk.

"Off the record and unofficially, Baumann, you and Steinberg did a hell of a job. Just do it nice and legal next time, do it the army way, OK? Dismissed."

In early December of 1945 I got lucky. I was one of seven ACEs, from a total seven hundred and fifty of us, chosen by merit of their work to spend ten days of leave at the French Riviera. Our destination was the Carlton Hotel in Cannes. I was not prepared for the splendor that we encountered there, especially not so soon after the war.

Because of our civilian status we were treated like officers, and ranking ones at that. Enlisted personnel had to spend their leave in Nice, not exactly chopped liver, but nevertheless not on a par with Cannes. There is no other way to describe it, for ten days we lived like millionaires.

In the evenings we went to the Martinez, another luxury hotel, with the largest bar and ballroom I had ever seen. I found out that I could call home from their switchboard as long as it was an official military call. That was certainly not he case with mine. But this was my chance. I could not phone London at all from my duty station in Germany.

Just in case the Martinez line was being monitored I decided on a little subterfuge. I went into a lobby phone booth and asked for a military line.

"Hello, this is Captain Barker speaking from the Martinez. Official military call. Give me Marseilles base. Hello Marseilles? Give me Paris base please. Hello Paris? Give me U.K. base."

"Is this an official call sir?" "Yes it is!"

"Just one minute please sir." "Hello U.K. base? Give me Speedwell 9492. Hello, mom?"

Easy, wasn't it? A bit childish maybe, but as I found out, I was not the only perpetrator. Anyway, it made my mother extremely happy. It was the first time in months that she heard my voice.

The bar at the Martinez was a great place to pick up Mademoiselles. They saw in me an American officer who spoke French. I was not about to dissuade them from that impression. Especially not a certain young lady whose name was Monique. Ah Monique!

The two girls sat at a table near the bar, obviously scoping out the scene. Indeed, so were we, my newly acquired friend Capt. Darryl Hanson and I, two guys just as obviously on the make.

Capt. Hanson, who liked to be called Tex, was on leave from 6th Corps, U.S. Cavalry, the original Anzio invasion troops. It was his second to the last night before he had to report back for duty.

In less time than it took to order a bottle of champagne we became a foursome.

Monique DelaCroix, the young lady I picked as my date for the evening, spoke very little English but her friend Nicole Gautier seemed fairly fluent, so it was only natural that Capt. Tex favored her.

Monique wore her chestnut brown hair in an upsweep, her eyes were almost black, she had a slightly irregular gallic nose, her high cheekbones sported a little rouge, but the overall impression was that of a sexy French tart, not that I mean that in a bad way.

Nicole was a blonde, Bridgit Bardot type. I am familiar with the old country song lyrics that state 'all the girls get prettier at closing time', but that really wasn't the case here. We had lucked into meeting two of Cannes' prettiest locals.

The champagne arrived at our table and we were ready to let the fun begin. And what a fun night it was!

When the band played *In The Mood*, Glen Miller's theme song, they sounded almost as good as the original. I am not much of a dancer, having spent too much time on bandstands making music for others, but with Monique in my arms I forgot all about that. I probably danced more that night than I ever have before or since.

When midnight rolled around and the orchestra played *Goodnight Ladies*, Monique and I strolled hand in hand onto the hotel veranda overlooking the Mediterranean. From there we watched moonlight beams reflecting on the gentle breakers lapping the shore. I know this all sounds overly romantic and it probably was. But that's how I remember it.

I walked Monique home the three blocks from the hotel to her apartment and she invited me in. I was sure I wouldn't have to utter that old chestnut phrase, '*voulez vous couche avec mois?*'

I knew she did.

Monique excused herself to go the bathroom, which gave me time to undress. I climbed into her bed and barely had time to put on a government-issue condom before she came out of the bathroom, wearing the flimsiest of negligees. Then, for the first time in my life, I made love to a real live girl, and a sexy French one at that.

With each stroke her moans of pleasure became more intense. "N'arete pas," she gasped, "don't stop!" Monique was enjoying this as much as I was, and I was the source of her pleasure. Years of frustration melted away at this moment. I imagined Adam must have felt like this, the first time he 'knew' Eve, as the Bible puts it. Be that the case or not, I was in my own paradise. And then it happened.

I felt something snap and realized with horror that the rubber had broken. I pulled out in a panic, much to Monique's displeasure. I felt myself break into a cold sweat.

"Monique, the rubber broke!" I gasped.

"Ca ne fait rien, Cheri, you 'ave more, nest ce pas?"

But I was through for the night. I was sure that in that one unguarded split second I had contracted some dreadful venereal disease, probably syphilis.

I knew all about that disease. When my father was a young man he contracted syphilis from a casual date with a young girl who worked in a Berlin flower shop. In those days, before the discovery of penicillin, the only available cure, and not a surefire one, was mercury, injected into the bloodstream. It was not until 1943 that penicillin, the so-called wonder drug, got used widely in the treatment of sexually transmitted diseases. As a matter of fact I remember during the war seeing huge posters depicting a sex siren wearing next to nothing on one half, and a syringe sporting a wicked needle on the other. The legend read: ONE NIGHT WITH VENUS MAY MEAN A LIFETIME WITH MERCURY.

But mercury could have a devastating effect on various organs of the body, mainly the heart. My father underwent blood tests every six months for a period of time to check for a recurrence of the disease, especially after he proposed to my mother. Before the two got married, he was declared cured. The effect on his heart however became clear only after he died at the young age of 49. His was not a regular type of heart attack but one caused by the damage from mercury.

I rushed back to my hotel and asked the officer in charge for the location of the nearest Pro Station. When I arrived there in near panic, the medics had me wash myself thoroughly with disinfectant and handed me a small tube of ointment. I was told to I squeeze the contents into the small opening of the offending member. It caused considerable discomfort. But that was nothing compared to the mental anguish I underwent for the next six weeks, praying that no tell tale rash would appear. Needless to say it was six weeks of total abstinence. As it turned out, I was lucky. Monique was clean.

8

Back in Germany our unit was transferred from Munich to Esslingen, a steel-manufacturing town near Stuttgart. Our HQ moved into the former Index Werke, a factory that had produced airplane parts for the Luftwaffe. Our divisional newspaper now had a proper name, The Index Indicator. In Munich our efforts ended up merely on a mimeographed sheet. Now I contracted with a local printer to produce a weekly four-page sheet on slick newsprint. I had a part-time staff of writers, artists and editors who volunteered their services. Some of them had actually been journalists in civilian life. I was the editor, but I found myself taking pictures for publication for the first time. I didn't know then that this would become a lifetime career. As before, the paper was only part of my duties. Running the club and looking after rest and recreation for the unit was still the major part.

When my sister announced a date for her wedding, I asked for and received a three-day emergency leave pass. Since my father was dead, I would be giving the bride away. We did have a guardian, Henry Loeb, a wonderful friend of the family who happened to be in the Wines and Spirit business. He wanted to take my dad's place, but my sister preferred that I play that role.

The wedding at our house included some four dozen guests. I set up a bar on a table by the bay windows facing the front, and stocked it, thanks to guardian Loeb, with a great variety of liquors.

As guests began to arrive I served as bartender, asking each guest what drink they wanted to toast my sister with. Of course I had to match their toast with a drink of my own. If they asked for a gin drink, I would drink gin. If their choice demanded whiskey, I would also pour one for me. If they drank champagne, I drank champagne. You get the idea. A friend of mine counted over twenty shots I guzzled that festive day.

After a while I felt a little dizzy, so I opened a window for some fresh air. As I leaned out of the window the inevitable happened. I vomited. The stream of barf landed in the front yard just as the officiating rabbi arrived. I don't know what effect it had on him, but I felt tremendously better. After the ceremony I stood up, facing the guests to give a speech I wrote for the occasion.

According to my mother, who was blissfully unaware of the barfing incident, I gave the speech perfectly, just the way I had rehearsed it. Once I concluded praising my sister, her new husband, wished them only the best in life, thanked the guests and should have sat down, I started anew.

"Ladies and Gentlemen," I began, my speech slurred, "I wanna give a speech."

That's as far as I got. I pitched forward, ramrod straight, like a tree felled in the forest, hitting the floor nose first. Someone should have yelled timber. They carried me upstairs to bed where I appeared to stop breathing.

As at about any Jewish wedding there were at least three doctors among the guests, two of which came upstairs to minister to me. I was in pretty bad shape. I not only had a severe case of alcoholic poisoning, my heart stopped beating, Dr. Levi gave me a shot of adrenaline directly into the heart. That saved my life.

My sister has not forgiven me to this day, and I, of course, gave up alcohol in all forms.

◆   ◆   ◆

"On a clear day you can see Brooklyn." There was a phrase I hadn't heard before.

It was a brisk winter morning in Esslingen the day after we arrived. You could see the snow on the mountains, but the sky was a brilliant blue. The young lady who made that remark stood in the mess hall chow line in front of me, waiting for a breakfast of powdered eggs and cold toast. The alternative was some none too appetizing looking oatmeal, which had the consistency of potato soup.

"And where would one have to stand to see Brooklyn?" I asked.

"Why, at Toity-Toid and Broadway, where else? You with the new group? When did you get in?"

"Late last night. By the way I'm Fred, Fred Baumann."

"Celia Weinstein. Come sit with me, I'll dish you all the dirt you need to know."

We sat down at a table and took stock of each other. Celia was wearing a neatly pressed uniform, starch collared shirt, with small gold US insignias in each lapel, and an officers cap tilted at a rakish angle, which she had not bothered to remove.

"If I may be so bold," I started up the conversation, "I have to tell you that you are one of the prettiest WDEs I've yet met, and its not just the uniform, although that makes you look extra snazzy."

"You only say that because its true," she shot back.

That was another phrase not in my vocabulary. This girl was something else. Standing about five foot three, dark hair, dark eyes, and charming to a fault, she may have been a little 'saftig'. But if she carried a couple of extra pounds, she carried them in very becoming curves.

"You're not so bad looking yourself," she teased, "ever tried to get in the movies?"

Now where had I heard that before?

"Flattery will get you anything. Are you flirting with me?"

"I'll have you know I'm a happily married woman."

"Your husband here with you?"

"No, he stayed back in New York."

"What line of work is he in?"

"He manufactures campaign buttons and badges, also other novelty items."

"He didn't mind you coming over here? How long did you sign up for?"

"Eighteen months, but I'll get to see him on leave. They're giving me two."

"So why did you come?"

"The government needed me. Somebody has to do it." Celia got up from the table. "I better get to work now. Would you like to come to my apartment for coffee and cookies this afternoon? Say four o'clock. It'll be strictly on the up and up. Just think of me as your local Welcome Wagon lady. Here, let me draw you a map. Mine is No. 4, the one on the left, first floor."

She walked away before I could give her an answer. We both knew what it would be. I always was a sucker for cookies.

Celia's apartment had the feeling of home. Frilly curtains on the kitchen windows, drapes in the sitting room, throw rugs on the floor and pictures on the walls.

"Coffee is brewing," she said after letting me in and taking my coat. "This is real Folgers, none of that mess hall swill. Make yourself comfortable, I'll bring the cookies in a sec."

"That's quite a place you have here," I said, as I walked around admiring the little homey touches she had added. There were flowers on the table, throw pillows on the couch and two lighted candles on the fireplace mantle. Yes, she actually had a fireplace with burning logs.

"They tell me it belonged to a Gauleiter before we liberated it," Celia explained. "Fellow had pretty good taste except for the portrait of Hitler over the mantle. That was gone when I got here. Too bad, I would have loved to crap all over it, pardon my French."

I tried to form a mental picture of Celia doing just that and began to laugh. Celia came in with a tin of chocolate chip cookies.

"Whats so funny, sonny?"

"The image you just painted. Hey! Chocolate chip, my favorite, how did you know?"

"What man doesn't like chocolate chip cookies? Enjoy, they're to die for. Now I want you to tell me all about yourself. In fifteen words or less! I gotta short attention span."

"Very funny! I'd rather hear your life story, even if it takes all night. Especially if it takes all night!

"Fresh! I told you I'm a happily married lady."

"Yes, but an adorable, temporarily unencumbered, gorgeous one."

"I bet you've said that to all the girls you've slept with."

"I would have had to say it in French, and then only once. I'm almost too embarrassed to admit this, but until last week I was a virgin."

"Come on, you're pulling my leg." Celia looked incredulous. "A good-looking mug like you? The girls should have been all over you."

"I may be old fashioned, but when a girl says no, I take it to mean no."

"Incredible, I thought men like you were extinct."

It was getting dark outside. The fire was burning low and I asked Celia if she wanted me to add another log.

"Good thinking. Woodpiles outside the kitchen door. Say, I have an idea. Why don't I open a can of Dinty Moore Beef Stew and you have supper here. Can't be any worse than tonight's mess hall offering. They call it chipped beef on toast, but you known what the GIs call it? Shit on a Shingle."

Thus it came about that the self-same person who declared herself married and off limits at four in the afternoon, invited me into her bed at eight in the evening. Go figure. But boy, did I have a lot to learn!

We began our relationship as pupil and teacher. In a college catalogue it would have been listed as 'Intercourse 101'. My lack of experience showed in a myriad ways.

Right off the bat, on our first night, after we made love, I turned over to go to sleep. Bad move!

Celia shook me awake. "Darling, I enjoyed the sex, but it shouldn't be like, wham bang, thank you ma'am. A woman needs more than that. She needs to be held, caressed, whispered to. You'll have to learn that."

That was only the first lesson.

Foreplay, after-play, various positions, I was getting the full treatment. Not that I wasn't enjoying every moment. That, and the home-cooked meals, the weekend ski trips, visits to the local symphonies and operas, in my mind I was becoming a man of the world.

We spent most nights together, but in the interest of propriety I always left before four a.m. to return to my own digs. My roommate Herbie was happy to have the place for himself and his little peccadilloes.

In a letter to my mother I wrote that if Celia were fifteen years younger and not married I probably would propose to her.

Our relationship lasted four glorious months. Then she went on leave, back to New York and her husband. It was not the same when she returned. I guess she didn't like the idea of my seeing other women. Jesus Christ almighty, she was seeing another man, even it was her husband.

9

Fast-forward thirty odd years.

Ever since I moved to the States, I wondered what had become of my first real love, or should I say first consummated love. I lived on the West Coast, but from time to time, when in New York, I tried to look her up in the telephone directory, each time without success.

My wife knew all about Celia.

Although not thrilled about any woman I had bedded before marriage, my wife found it hard to protest when I told her, on several occasions, that if she considered me a good lover she had Celia to thank for it.

"I'd rather not talk about it," she would say, "besides, how would I know? You're the only man I've ever made love to."

I wanted to say, "Trust me on that score," but I knew when to shut up.

Coming home from a European trip one year, we happened to stay overnight at the Algonquin Hotel in New York. As I left the elevator and walked into the hotel lobby, I noticed a bookshelf out side the wooden phone booth holding several directories.

Then it hit me like the proverbial bolt from the blue.

All these years I had looked for Celia's phone number in the Manhattan directory. Here were five directories, one for each borough. Celia was from Brooklyn! I grabbed the Brooklyn phone book and presto, there she was, Celia Weinstein, 183 Ocean Park Avenue.

That was not the house number I had written in my little black book thirty years before, but it appeared to be in the same block. I informed my wife of my discovery and asked her if she minded my phoning Celia.

"Of course not, darling, go ahead," she agreed. "I don't think I have anything to fear from her. If Celia is still alive she has to be seventy if she's a day. But I don't want to meet her."

On the fourth ring a man answered the phone.

"Hello," I said, "I hope I am not disturbing you, but is this the Celia Weinstein residence?"

"Yes, who is calling?"

"My name is Fred Bauman, Mrs. Weinstein and I were stationed together in Germany in 1946. I've been trying to contact her for a while, but that's a long story."

"Oh yes, I think she told me about you, but she is not here. She's in Israel. My wife spends six months of the year there. She'll be back in October."

I was beginning to have serious doubts about Celia. Obviously she stayed married to the same man all these years, but back then she spent eighteen month away from him in Germany, and now, six months of the year in Israel.

"Well thank you very much. You might want to tell her I called, and Ill try again in October."

I hung up and related the conversation to my wife.

"Strange woman that," she opined, "you really want to get in touch with her again? It's your choice, I don't care one way or the other."

As luck would have it, my newspaper was sending me to New York in November. I was to cover a local high school band marching in Macys Thanksgiving parade. Once I knew at which hotel I would be staying, I phoned Celia again. This time she was home.

"Hi Celia, this is Fred Bauman calling from California," I began.

"Who? I don't know any Fred Bauman."

Was she kidding? Was she afraid her husband was monitoring the conversation? Did she have Alzheimer's? Was she some other Celia Weinstein? It was possible, but not probable.

"Celia, its Fred. CCD, Esslingen, Have you forgotten?"

"Freddy? Freddy from London?" She sounded taken aback.

"The very same. How are you, Celia, how's life been treating you?"

"What are you doing in this country? You say you are in California? What are you doing there?"

"I've lived in America for over thirty years. I'm a newspaper photographer."

"Thirty years, and now you're calling me?"

"I feel like a goddamned fool confessing this, Ceel, but I could never find your phone number in the Manhattan directory."

"Of course you couldn't, stupid, I'm in the Brooklyn book."

"I didn't find that out until last month. Scouts honor. I know that sounds stupid, but it never occurred to me that each borough has its own directory. Listen Celia, I'll be in New York around Thanksgiving. I'd sure like to see you."

"I'm looking forward to that too." She chuckled. "Little Freddy from London, has it really been thirty years?"

"Thirty-two to be precise."

I told Celia which hotel I would be staying in and the approximate time of arrival.

Prior to coming to New York I had business in St. Louis. On arrival there I learned a blizzard had just breezed through. The next day there was two feet of snow on the ground. I was not sure my plane to New York could take off on time, but after an hours delay we made it.

When I checked into my hotel I still hadn't thawed out. I decided to take a nice, hot, leisurely bath. I had barely started to soak, finally getting warm, when the phone rang in my room. It was Celia.

"Hi, Celia, you've caught me with my clothes off, I'm taking a bath. Where are you calling from?"

"The hotel lobby."

"Oh?" I was a little shocked. I had not planned to see her until dinnertime. "Give me a few minutes and Ill come down to get you."

"That's not necessary, Ill sit here a few and give you time to dress. Then I'll come up."

I was beginning to think this whole thing was a mistake. What would Celia look like after all these years? Why was she so eager to see me? What had she told her husband? On the other hand, why was I worried. What could a seventy-year old woman do to me? I dried off and dressed in a hurry.

I was barely in time. There was a knock at the door.

I went to open it, and at that instant, for the first time, I came face to face with my own mortality.

Whatever mental image I held of the beautiful woman who taught me how to make love disappeared in a flash.

Standing before me was this wrinkled little old nebbish dressed in black, the right side of her face showing hints of Bells palsy, mouth slightly droopy, trying her best to greet me with a big smile. How long would it be before I was ravaged by old age?

I hugged her affectionately nevertheless. "Come into my parlor, said the spider to the fly," I teased.

"You shudda stayed in the tub," Celia grinned, "I could have scrubbed your back."

My room had a small table and two chairs by the window.

"Come and sit down," I said, "make yourself at home."

Celia took off her gloves, scarf and coat as well as a small cloche hat and threw them on the bed. As she did, something rolled out of her hat.

"What is that?" I asked, pointing to the mysterious little bundle.

"A spare set of pantyhose," she explained, not the least phased. "You know, just in case!

Just in case of what? Did she really think I would tear off her underclothes so we could make mad passionate love? For a moment I was at a loss what to do next. Thank God I had my camera with me.

"Let me take some pictures of you," I suggested. "You know that's my profession now. I will make you look glamorous."

"I brought a whole bunch from our days in Europe," she said, reaching into her purse to pull out a stack of snapshots. "If you see any you like they're yours. They're dupes. I sure would like to have any of us you might still have around."

We spent the next half an hour looking at a long forgotten past whose erstwhile magic had disappeared. Back then we were two different people. Thomas Wolfe was right, you can't go home again.

It was almost too early to eat, but I was anxious to leave the room.

We were the only couple in the hotel dining room, which had just opened for dinner.

"How did you get here?" I asked, "by taxi?"

"No, my husband brought me."

"Your husband? Where is he now, waiting outside in the car?"

"Don't be silly, he's gone on his own date. He'll come and get me later."

Oh lord, I thought, how much later?

"Don't get me wrong, Celia, but I got to ask you this: What kind of marriage have you had all these years? I mean here you are with me, your husband is with a girl friend, you spend half the year in Israel, why did you stay married?"

"I guess you'd call it a marriage of convenience. Neither of us believes in divorce, we get along with each other and we each do what we want. Hard to beat, huh?"

It was almost eleven when Celia's husband finally picked her up. We had gone back to my room and I had a hard time staying awake, making forced conversation. Celia said she wouldn't mind it a bit if I went to bed, but that was the last thing on my mind. I could just see the headlines in the morning papers:

55-YEAR OLD MAN HAS HEART ATTACK FIGHTING
OFF RAPE BY 70-YEAR OLD WOMAN!

10

Be kind rewind, back to 1946.

All good things have to end. After Celia and I broke up I had several girl friends but I approached any new relationship from a far more pragmatic point of view. I had the experience but probably lacked the maturity for any serious relationship. Besides, I was having too much fun, like the day I picked up a hitchhiker on my way from Stuttgart to Heidelberg. I had business to take care of in the beautiful Neckar country.

Hitchhiking was an accepted mode of transportation in those days, not only for the locals, whose access to cars and gasoline was severely limited, but also for GIs who were not as fortunate as I was with my government issued jeep.

I almost did not stop when I saw her standing by the side of the Autobahn, a slender, well-dressed young lady with a small suitcase at her feet. Although I had frequent contacts among German nationals due to the nature of my work, fraternization was still somewhat frowned on. The image I saw in my rear view mirror made me stop and back up. Not only was this hitchhiker very pretty, she had a certain regal bearing about her, an indefinable something that aroused my curiosity.

"Where to?" I asked in German as my jeep came to a halt.

"Heidelberg," she answered in English, "may I hitch a ride? I'd appreciate it."

This was no ordinary German peasant girl, this was a highly educated individual, culture oozing from every pore.

"Hop in, throw your suitcase in the back," I said, glad that I had stopped for her.

Although her knee-length skirt, robins egg blue blazer and turtleneck sweater looked elegant, on closer inspection they were beginning to show some wear. I noticed that the blazer had what appeared to be a family crest on its breast pocket.

"What's that on your blazer?" I asked. "Is it a family crest?"

"Yes, as a matter of fact, that's been our family crest for a couple of hundred years."

"Really, are you a member of the nobility?"

"If you want to call it that, though it hasn't done us much good lately."

"Tell me your name."

"Dorothea."

"Dorothea what?"

"Dorothea von Schaefer Tettau Tolk."

"That's quite a mouthful. What are you going to Heidelberg for?"

"My aunt has an estate there, I'm going to live with her for a while."

I had become so fascinated with Dorothea's story, I couldn't for the life of me tell you if we were holding our conversation in English or German. This hitchhiker turned out to be one Baroness von Schaefer Tettau-Tolk whose father, a Wehrmacht general, had been killed on the Russian front and whose mother had died in an air raid on Dresden. After struggling to manage on her own she decided her aunt could help her get back on her feet.

It was getting dark as we arrived in Heidelberg. I pulled up in front of the small hotel serving as BHQ and asked Dorothea to wait in the jeep while I checked matters inside. I had promised her a hot bath if possible, something she had not been able to enjoy for quite a while.

The sergeant at the front desk gave me a brisk salute, checked my travel orders and gave me the key to my room.

"I know this is against regulations, sergeant," I began with some hesitation, "but I have a young lady with me, a civilian, and I'm wondering if she could perhaps come up and take a hot bath?"

I had brought a carton of cigarettes along and put it on the desk. On the black market that would fetch a sergeant's pay for a month.

"I have no use for these, and I wondered......"

The sergeant put my cigarettes under the desk and gave me a wink.

"Gotta check up on some paper work in the back, sir," he explained. "Take me about five minutes. And, ahem, be sure to have her out of here before eight a.m., sir, that's when the day shift comes on."

"Thank you sergeant, I really appreciate this."

"If you are hungry I have some K-rations with me," I told Dorothea when we got up into the room, "nothing to put on a table cloth, but edible."

"I'm starving, I'm sure they'll be wonderful," she said, "I haven't exactly been dining on haut cuisine the last few months."

When we were finished with the K-rations, Hershey bar and all, Dorothea asked if she could have the chewing gum neither of us had touched.

"I'd like to take these to my nephews," she said.

"You want to take your bath now?" I asked, then came right to the point.

"Listen, baroness, I do not want to force myself on you, but Id love it if you spent the night."

"I thought you'd never ask!" she laughed, "of course I'll stay. That's another thing I haven't done for quite a while. But don't call me baroness, that's the past."

We made love twice that night. Somehow I felt I was doing payback. Here was I, the little Jewish kid the Nazis wanted to kill, fucking a member of the German nobility. I'm willing to bet a year's pay that this young lady had never before seen a circumcised penis.

◆   ◆   ◆

With two months to go on my contract I was transferred again, this time to Kulmbach near the Czech border where the Russian zone of occupation began. I was to open a new CCD station, not so much for the censoring of mail, but rather to establish a listening post against our former Communist allies.

Once again I worked in Special Services. Our headquarters was in the Hornschuch Haus, an enormous mansion we confiscated from the owner, a Spinning Mill tycoon. We let him live in the gatekeeper lodge, which was bigger than any house I had ever lived in.

Our people had recently reactivated a bottling plant in Hof, a small town right on the Czech border. To stock the club bar I hitched a small trailer to my jeep and drove there to pick up a load of Coca Cola. I was forced to take a circuitous route since many of the roads were still pock-marked with artillery shell damage.

After loading up with a dozen cases of Coke I stopped on the way back to ask directions from a local, hoping he could tell me of a shortcut. He pointed me to a dirt road, which led through a forest.

"Ja, you go zere and that vill save you ten kilometers," he told me in broken English. "On other side is road to Kulmbach."

About five kilometers through this dense forest I became a little leery. I had a feeling something was wrong.

All of a sudden I heard rapid gunfire, and bullets ripped through the branches above my head.

That son-of-a-bitch had sent me right into the Russian zone.

I spun the wheel into a screeching U-turn around the nearest tree, almost tipping over the trailer. Several cases of Coke spilled out. I wasn't about to stop and pick them up. The Russians probably were shooting warning shots, or they would have killed me. Still, I did not return to the dirt road, hoping the trees would give me cover.

When I returned to Kulmbach I reported the incident to Military Government HQ, hoping they would send a platoon to shoot up the Ivans. No such luck!

"You should have stuck to the roads that got you there" a major told me. "We are not about to start another war!"

I hope the Russians enjoyed the Coke.

11

It was in Kulmbach that I met Elizabeth Davenport, an ex-WAVE who had become a WDE.

Born in D.C. but living in New York City when she enlisted in the Navy, Libby, as she liked to be called, was a blue-eyed blonde who could easily be mistaken for a movie star.

Although I was unfamiliar with the term then, she was a typical WASP beauty, the very opposite of the proverbial Jewish Princess I had been encouraged to seek out for my life partner. So, naturally, after knowing her for two weeks, I proposed. And kept on proposing. Finally, after two months, her maybes became yeses. On my last quick furlough to Paris I bought Libby an engagement ring and a gold watch for good measure. Now we were officially engaged. The only obstacle to our plans was the fact that my tour of duty was up six months before hers.

We agreed that I would return to my London home and wait for her. We would get married there. When I boarded a train for LeHavre and the ferry to Dover the next morning, it did not strike me as odd that Libby did not come to see me off. We had said our good-byes the night before. Although I slept in her bed, we did not have sex. I was saving that for the honeymoon.

Getting off the ferry we had to go through customs. No big deal, there was nothing to declare. With a duffel bag over my shoulder and dragging a suitcase, I waited in line for the next customs agent. I was wearing my American uniform and expected to be waved right through. The dour faced inspector looked me in the face—stared would be a better description and in a bored tone asked me the routine questions.

Where was I coming from? What was the last time I was in the United Kingdom? How long was I staying? The final thing he asked was if I had anything to declare.

"I don't believe so," I answered, fully believing that I spoke the truth.

"Very well Mr."—he looked at my identification papers before handing them back—"Mr. Baumann, enjoy your stay." He was about to pass me through to Immigration when he stopped.

"Oh, just one more thing, sir, would you mind opening that suitcase?"

"The suitcase? Sure."

I lifted it onto the counter and opened it up.

The inspector took a look and then, pointing to its content, asked: "What are those?"

Nestled right on top were a dozen suede leather gloves. They were a token present from the manager of a leather factory in Offenbach, which had once been owned by my father. I intended them as gifts for prospective girl friends and of course for my mother and sister.

Unfortunately, suede gloves were considered a luxury item subject to import duties. Actually I knew that. I should have declared them whether I paid for them or not.

"Would you mind stepping this way?" the customs man asked as he gestured for a uniformed guard to escort me. I was led out of the line into a small room and strip-searched. Another inspector came in with a form for me to sign.

"You are being charged with a customs violation," he intoned ominously. "The charge is smuggling. You will have to appear in court at a later date."

He held up the form and had me sign it.

"We are releasing you on your own cognizance," he explained. "You will be notified of your court date and I advise you to seek legal help."

What a homecoming that was. I was about to get a criminal record.

My widowed mother was overjoyed to have me home after a two-year absence. For the time being I kept my engagement a secret. Bringing a shiksa into the family would take a little preparation. The more immediate problem was my run-in with the law.

The summons came soon enough. My mother contacted the family lawyer who in turn recommended a barrister to defend me in court. I could have received jail time.

As it turned out, Rumpole for the Defense, as I like to think of him, painted such a sainted portrait of me, 'defender of the realm', 'Boy Scout', 'youngest air raid warden in Hertfordshire', 'kind to his mother', that I was surprised I didn't walk out of there scot-free. In the end I was fined fifty pounds, a goodly sum for those days, which my mother paid in addition to the hundred guineas charged by the barrister.

I wrote Libby almost every day, eagerly awaiting her replies.

They never came.

A month passed by, then two. The APO address to which I mailed my love letters was accurate. None were returned.

In desperation I wrote her commanding officer. That's when I got my Dear John letter. Not from her, I got one from him.

Miss Davenport doesn't care to correspond, he wrote. *In fact she wants nothing further to do with you. He was sorry to have to inform me of the facts, and under the circumstances would recommend that I look for greener pastures in my own country!*

I was devastated. There had to be some mistake! What girl would not want to marry someone as good-looking, charming and altogether nice? On top of that I was very funny.

There was just one solution:

I would have to go to New York to reunite with my beloved. I would, in fact, immigrate to the United States.

The fact that, other than her name, I knew nothing about Miss Elizabeth Davenport did not deter me. I knew nothing about her family, nothing about her address, I had no phone number, no names of friends or former employers, nothing, absolutely nothing! Except for one thing. She had given me a small snapshot of herself in a two-piece bathing suit, standing on the rooftop of her New York tenement.

The apartment building had twin water towers—most had only one—and visible in the background was part of a distinctive art deco office building shaped like layers of a wedding cake. Later I would learn that it was the McGraw-Hill Building. I would have to find that apartment and with it, her.

As luck would have it I had an uncle in New York who could provide me with the necessary affidavit and documents enabling me to carry out my plan. I asked him not to let my family in on our secret. My father had helped him get to America and this was how he could show his gratitude toward me. My plan was to let my mother know only one week before departure. I knew it would be a great shock, but why let her worry needlessly such a long time ahead?

When I finally told her she was near hysterics. My one saving grace was that she had remarried and I was no longer the man of the house. Still, I was sure her friends would judge me selfish and unfeeling.

It took several months, but on August 17th, 1947, I boarded TWA flight 2, London Heathrow to New York Idyllwild. That was the airport's name until it was changed to JFK.

Until I found a job and made some money I would be my uncle's guest. What I really wanted to find was Libby.

All I had to do now was to discover, from among thousands of Manhattan apartment building roofs, the one that matched the scene on my snapshot. Good luck!

My first task was to find a general location. Telling my uncle I was looking for work, I hit the streets and began showing my photo to cops and cabbies, the most likely sources to solve that part of the puzzle.

It proved easier than I thought. There was a general consensus about the McGraw-Hill building, a well-known landmark on the Manhattan skyline.

"That's gotta be the McGraw to be sure," an Irish member of New York's Finest told me when I showed him the snapshot, "and that's the Hudson on the left there," he said pointing to the top left corner of the photo. "Your apartment's probably on the lower West Side.

Then he made another educated guess. I loved that cop. "Judging by the distance to the McGraw," he explained, "your place should be between West 28th and 39th Streets."

Having that information should limit my search.

"That must be some fine lass you're chasing," were the cops parting words.

Now the hard part began.

I started climbing rooftops to look toward mid-town, in hopes of recognizing the scene in my photo. Some buildings I could just enter, take the elevator to the top if there was an elevator, and look for stairs to the roof.

Other buildings had suspicious supers who had to be convinced I was not intending to jump. Small bribes often helped.

I must have climbed a hundred rooftops. Some days I came close. There would be the McGraw but only a solitary water tower. The few apartments that boasted twin towers did not line up with the art deco structure.

After two weeks I was ready to give up. Had it all been in vain? Had I left my home and family for nothing? Was I just a stupid love-struck fool?

But then, on the fifteenth day of my quest, Eureka, there it was! On a gloriously sunny September morning I found the exact composition. The unmistakable twin towers, the McGraw-Hill in the back right, Hudson River to the left.

There was no girl on the roof, of course, but soon she would be there, and I would take her picture.

Ten minutes later I was at the front stoop of a four-story, gray, weather worn tenement building on West 32nd Street, a half block from Tenth Avenue. These days that building is gone. It was razed to make room for the Jacob Javitz Convention Center.

In typical New York fashion, the landlady was leaning out of her ground floor apartment, her ample bosom resting on the windowsill.

I explained what I was doing there and asked for Libby's apartment number. Her answer just about floored me.

"Miss Davenport ain't due back until tomorrow," she informed me as she reached into her pocket to pull out a crumpled sheet of paper. "I got her letter right here. You a friend of hers?"

More than six months had passed since I left Libby in Germany. I had spent two weeks searching for her apartment, yet incredibly, I had beaten her home by a day.

Wanting to give Libby a chance to settle back in, I decided not to return the following day but wait for the weekend.

On Saturday at nine o'clock in the morning I climbed the three floors to her apartment and knocked on the door. My heart pounded as the door opened. There she stood, my fiancée, in the flesh. She looked like she was about to faint. But she recovered.

"My God, what are you doing here in New York?" she gasped. "How did you find me? How long have you been in the States?"

Answering the questions in order, I told her my story, anticipating right from the start that it would not have a happy ending. I asked what had happened to the ring, the watch and a pair of custom crafted skis I left with her. Turns out she hocked them all.

Libby invited me in and asked if she could fix breakfast, "You have to leave right after," she warned, "my husband will be returning from running some errands."

My fiancée had a husband!

I never got to eat breakfast.

The husband, a burly ex-Marine, came home sooner than expected. In a menacing tone he asked who the hell I was. When I informed him in my fine British public school accent that I was Miss Davenports fiancée, he gave a sarcastic laugh and told me that he was her—expletive deleted—husband. Then he grabbed me by the scruff of the neck like a nightclub bouncer and threw me half a flight down the stairs.

My feelings were hurt a lot more than my body. Staying in New York was out of the question now. I had to get away.

12

Taking stock of my life found me wanting in any trade or occupation. I had no college degree, no experience along any line, I was alone in a strange country, for which I had no one to blame except myself. But I was young, and I had chutzpah.

Why not set my sights on journalism? I had a modicum of background knowledge. I was the editor of divisional army rag, though any grade school paper could have run rings around us. Never mind. I would advertise my talents in the trade publication *Editor & Publisher*.

Since most returning servicemen were taking advantage of the GI Bill to attend college, there was a shortage of reporters, especially at the starting level. My ad, which may have been slightly exaggerated as to my qualifications, drew no less than twenty-eight replies. There was one drawback. Of the twenty-eight, all but three asked for my religious affiliation. Hard as it is to believe today, many newspapers did not hire Jews, or at least, had a strict quota. If you were black you stood almost no chance.

One of the three papers was the Denison (Tex) Herald. They were looking for a combination reporter/photographer. Press photographers used the 4x5 Speed Graphic camera almost exclusively. A smaller format camera was not deemed suitable for newsprint reproduction. I had never even held a Speed Graphic in my hand, let alone knew how to use it.

A few days after the offer arrived from Denison I found myself riding the subway from my uncle's home on 121st Street to Times Square. I can't remember what my agenda was that day, but I do recall vividly what happened when the train stopped at 82nd St. A mother and daughter came aboard, and I rose to offer my seat to the mother.

The fact that her daughter was drop dead gorgeous had nothing to do with my acting like a gentleman. If you believe that I have a bridge I would like to sell you.

"Why thank you very much, young man," the mother said, "you don't see many New Yorkers giving up their seats."

"I'm not a New Yorker, ma'am, I am from London, England. It's quite the usual thing there."

I turned to the daughter. "Excuse me for asking, but haven't I seen your picture in a magazine? I know that sounds corny, but I could almost swear to it."

"You probably have, LIFE magazine has a group of us in the current issue. They have a story on the Miss America pageant."

"And you're Miss America, right?" I didn't doubt it for a second.

"Not quite, I'm Miss Texas of 1947. But I was named Miss Congeniality."

"Really? Congratulations. Whats your name?"

"I'm Lynn McClain, from Lufkin Texas."

"Now how's that for a coincidence? I'm headed to Texas. Going to work for a newspaper."

I said it even though I had not been hired yet. But now I was keener than ever to get the job.

"Momma, this man is coming to Texas, how about that? Doesn't he have a cute accent?"

"Well give him our address, Lynn honey," she said, "Y'all come to see us now. Did you tell Lynn your name?"

"No, I'm Fred Bauman, pleased to meet you Mrs. McClain. I certainly will try to visit."

Lynn wrote her name and address on a piece of paper and handed it to me. The train came to stop at Times Square. I said farewell and got off.

The moment the subway doors closed behind me I realized just how stupid I was. Here I get to meet Miss Texas in New York, I am trying to get hired by a Texas paper, and I let an exclusive interview slip right through my fingers. But all was not lost.

There was a Western Union office a few doors from the subway exit. What is it they used to say about rapid communication before the advent of the Internet? Telephone, telegraph, or tell a woman!

I sent a telegram to the address Lynn had given me.

FOUND POCKETBOOK BELONG LYNN MCCLAIN stop PLEASE WIRE NEW YORK ADDRESS C/O WESTERN UNION TIMES SQUARE stop WILL AWAIT YOUR ANSWER.

In a little over an hour my crazy effort was rewarded. Back came a telegram from Lynn's grandparents in Lufkin.

LYNN'S ADDRESS IS 3421 78 ST JACKSON HEIGHTS LONG ISLAND CARE MRS A H HEATON.

Now I grabbed the bull by the horn. I went to Schrafts, the famous candy store, and purchased a fake pocket book filled with a variety of Schrafts candies. I also bought a dozen red roses.

Around four o'clock that afternoon I presented myself at the Long Island address. It was the second time in a week that I arrived unannounced at a woman's apartment. This time it had a much happier ending.

"I've come to see Lynn," I told the lady who answered the door. "You must be Mrs. Heaton?"

Mrs. Heaton turned out to be Lynn's aunt. I handed her the flowers.

"These are for you ma'am, for crashing the party. I hope I'm not intruding."

By this time both Lynn and her mother had appeared in the entrance hallway, mouths agape. I quickly explained why I was there and handed Lynn the candy.

"I hope this makes up for the little white lie in the telegram," I pleaded. "I've come here for an interview."

The interview was a success. I sent it airmail express to the Denison Herald along with a cover letter explaining the circumstances: Boy meets girl, boy loses girl, boy finds girl, boy gets interview.

A week later I received my second telegram in America, this time not in Times-Square but at my uncle's residence in Washington Heights.

REPORT FOR WORK OCTOBER 1st.

It was from Fred Conn, publisher of the Denison (Tex) Herald. They ran the story under my byline even before I started working there.

◆   ◆   ◆

As much as my mother hated to see me leave England, and as vehemently opposed as she was to my choice, she would not let me go as a penniless immigrant. She gave me one thousand British pounds, which I shamelessly accepted, but accepted never the less. Converted into dollars at the then rate of exchange, that translated into a cool four-thousand bucks. Within a year the money would be gone.

Before boarding the train for Texas I bought a copy of the *Graflex/Graphic* book of photography to acquaint myself with the workings of their press cameras. The book cost five dollars, expensive, but necessary. I read it cover to cover. By the time I reached my destination I had become an expert on press photography. Yeah, right!

I began work the day after I arrived. For the first week I stayed in the Hotel Denison, the only hotel in town, other than a few small motels. Then the classified ads staff helped me find a small apartment within walking distance of the job.

The environment of a small Texas town in the middle of the Bible belt was bound to give me culture shock.

I prided myself on being open minded and capable of adjusting to almost any circumstance. The first time I saw two water fountains a couple of yards apart with signs over them stating 'Whites Only', and 'Coloreds', I could hardly believe my eyes. After all, slavery had been abolished over three quarters of a century ago.

The first time I bought breakfast at Joe's Coffee Shop, I paid the check at the register and started to walk out. I thought I heard owner, Joe, call me back. I turned around and stood by the counter wondering what Joe wanted from me. When he ignored my presence I walked out again. Again I heard him say it: Y'all come back now! I returned to the cash register a second time.

This time I asked him why he kept calling me back. Joe laughed so hard I thought he would have a stroke. The story quickly made the rounds. Folks teased me about it, but in a Texas friendly way. I didn't mind. It helped me in my reporting assignments. I was no longer a stranger to be suspicious of.

Denison was in a dry county, meaning no liquor could be served or sold. Since I didn't drink following the disaster at my sisters wedding, I didn't much care. If I had, there were always the bootleggers.

Came election time, when the wet/dry choice was voted on, there was a strange alliance between the bible thumping, temperance preaching ministers and the bootleggers. Talk about politics making strange bedfellows! Each had a similar goal. Keep the county dry, good for business, good for religion.

No one seemed to care about the hypocrisy of the thing. One of my first assignments at the Herald was covering the local prohibition election. Mr. McManus, I forget his first name, a deacon in the First Baptist Church and owner of a Men's clothing store was the leader of the 'Drys'. Campaign headquarters was in his house. This time around, the pro liquor people were doing a lot better than the last time. Mr. McManus was worried. Toward midnight, with the vote count almost complete, it looked fairly even. First one side was ahead by a few votes, then the other.

The final count came in at last. Once again, but only by a slim margin, the Drys had won.

Mr. McManus gathered his campaign workers in his private den.

"Time to celebrate folks," he enthused, "name your poison." He slid a section of a bookcase aside to reveal a liquor cabinet. In it were almost as many different brands of liquor as at my sisters wedding. That part of the story did not make the paper. I knew better than to write it.

Things were not going well for me at the paper. I had learned how to take and develop 4x5 pictures, thanks only to the kindness of a fellow photographer. Her name was Jackie Nodler. She was a graduate of the Missouri School of Journalism, one of the finest in the country. She recognized my shortcomings immediately but took me under her wing. Literally! Jackie stood six foot tall, skinny as a rail not a spare ounce of fat on her body, yet to me she was a beautiful golden angle.

With the lights turned off in the darkroom, she made me stand behind her and told me to put my arms around her, my hands on top of hers. This way I felt how she shuffled the 4x5 pieces of film in the developer tray and transferred them from there to the stop bath and hypo.

Bigger papers had tanks and film-holders. We were more primitive. It was the perfect way to learn, and no matter how many boy/girl in a darkroom jokes come to mind, there was absolutely nothing even remotely erotic about the experience.

I shall forever be grateful to Jackie. She kept my lack of photography knowledge secret from my boss. But that was not my only problem.

I knew practically nothing about journalism, and that was becoming more obvious all the time. The day I asked Claude Easterly, our editor, what 30 meant at the end of a page of copy, I probably sealed my fate.

Jack Ingram, our 16-year old copyboy, whom I had befriended and whose family socialized with Easterly, was the bearer of bad tidings.

"Hate to tell you this," Jack confided to me shortly after my second month at the Herald, "you're going to get fired. Claude says you didn't exactly tell the truth when Fred Conn hired you."

That was part of the problem. Claude Easterly was on vacation when Conn sent me that telegram. Being on the business, rather than the news side of the paper, his reading of my story and cover letter probably was more enthusiastic than it should have been.

The morning after Jack informed me of my doom, I showed up at Claude's office at seven in the morning. Claude was always the first to arrive and last to leave. This morning I beat him by three minutes. He looked surprised when he saw me.

"I understand you are going to fire me, sir," I began. "I realize that I was hired on somewhat false pretenses and I apologize for that. But I desperately need this job. I am willing to work day and night if you will teach me the ropes. I promise you will not be sorry."

I might also have said something about being all alone, a stranger in a strange country, although it was a somewhat traumatic experience, so I don't remember everything.

"Well, I actually was thinking of letting you go, but I admire your guts." Easterly seemed impressed. "And yes, I am willing to teach you. Let this be a new start. Everyone deserves a second chance."

I stayed on and learned. I could not have had a better teacher. When I left the Herald a year later to go to college, Claude assured me that there would always be a job open for me at his paper as long as he was editor.

"I've never met anyone who worked a hard as you did to succeed," he told me. Better yet, he put it in writing.

My year at the Herald, working for thirty-five dollars a week, was the last of my carefree existence for a while. When I started there, I still had over three thousand dollars in my bank account.

The first major purchase I made was a car. It was not a new car, it was a used model, or as they say today, 'previously owned'. In 1947, so short a time after the end of the war, cars were still hard to come buy, new or used. Unfortunately the dealer saw me coming. I paid $750 for a 1936 Chevrolet Coupe, which should have sold for under $500.

My apartment was another drain on the pocket book. A furnished room should have done the trick. Instead I hired a black maid to come in twice a week.

Next I bought some clothes. Not just any clothes. My friend from the local option election, Mr. McManus, sold me an expensive Texas style gabardine tan suit. With it came tooled leather cowboy boots bearing the Fry label. To top it all off, literally, I bought a ten-gallon Stetson. Now I was a real Texan. Until I opened my mouth. Then I got called a bloody limey. I tried hard to shed my British accent. When I did, they called me a Damned Yankee.

In the South, that's worse than being a Bloody Limey.

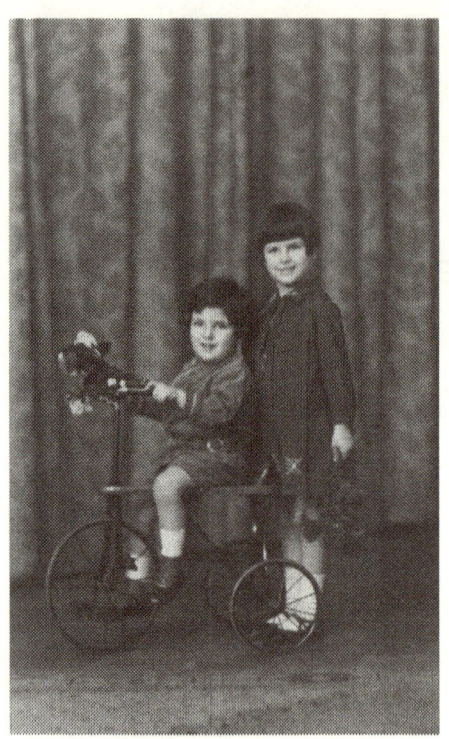

"Fritzchen" with sister Lili in their
Berlin apartment

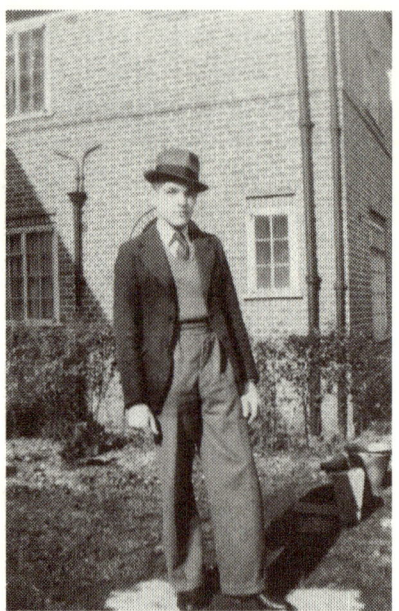

A snappy dresser outside London
home at age 16

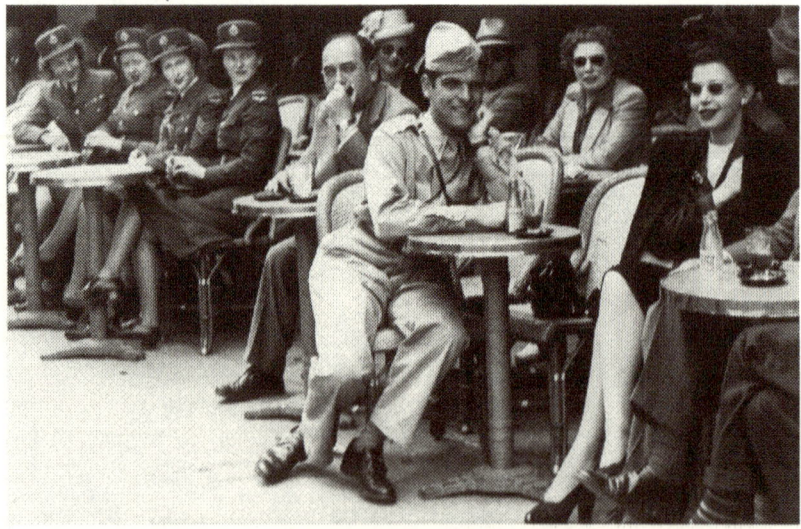

On leave in Paris, 1945. What are all those ladies looking at?

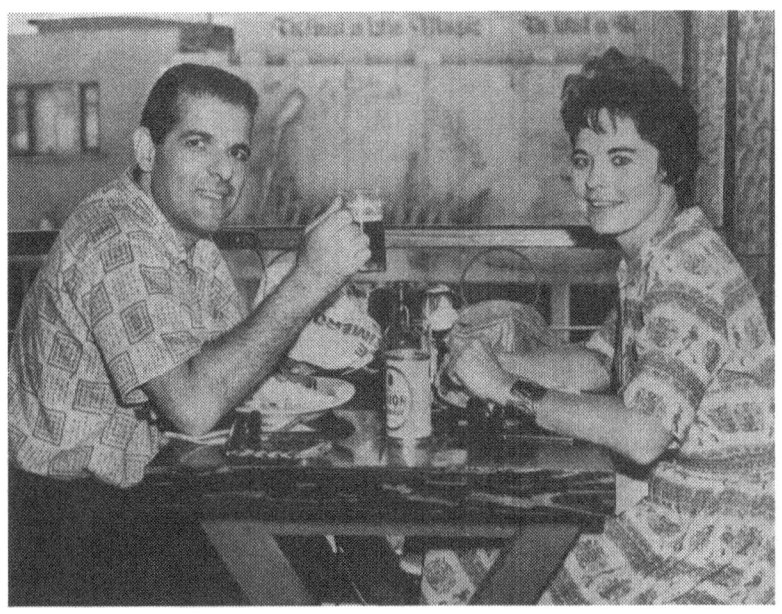

With wife Vivian on their first trip to Mexico

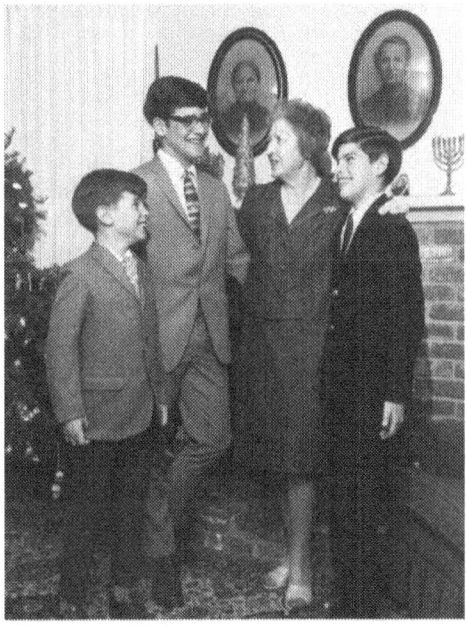

Sons Marc, Guy, and David with grandmother Regi Baumann

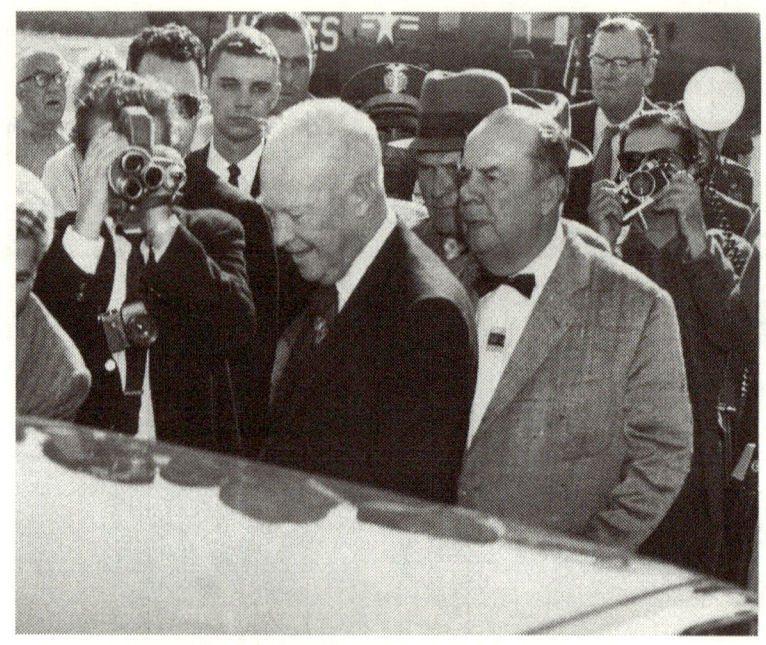

Covering President Eisenhower in Texas. I'm at far right.

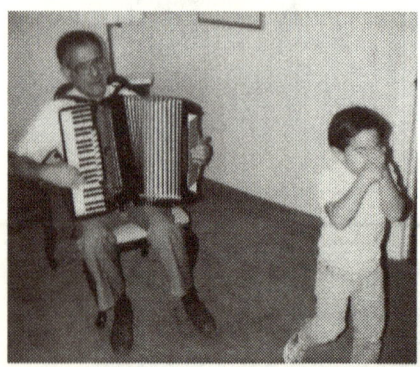

Accordion players are never appreciated, but my own nephew?

The offending Xmas card photo. I wonder why?

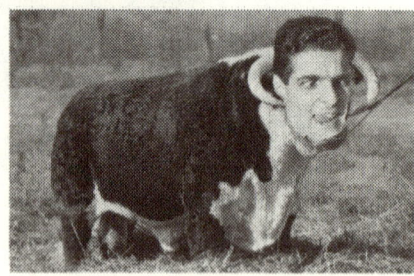

Right: On assignment with the U.S. Air Force

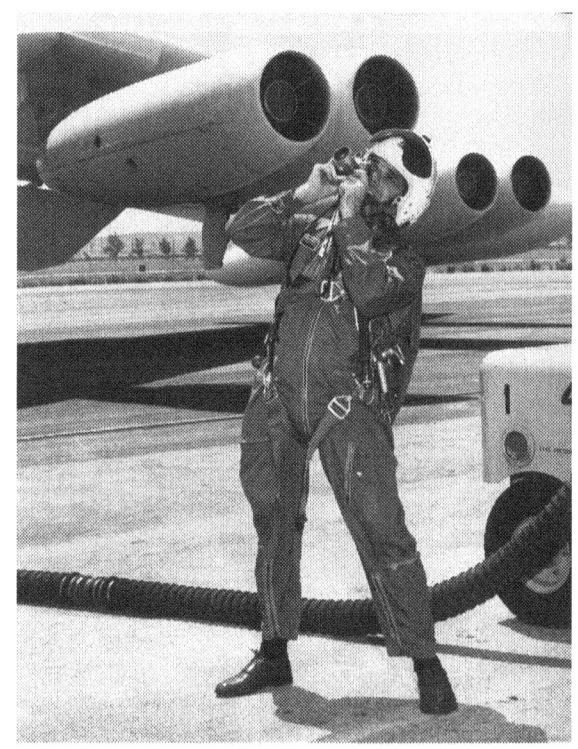

Bottom left: Father and son covering Prince Philip in Palm Springs

Bottom right: As a young college student in Texas

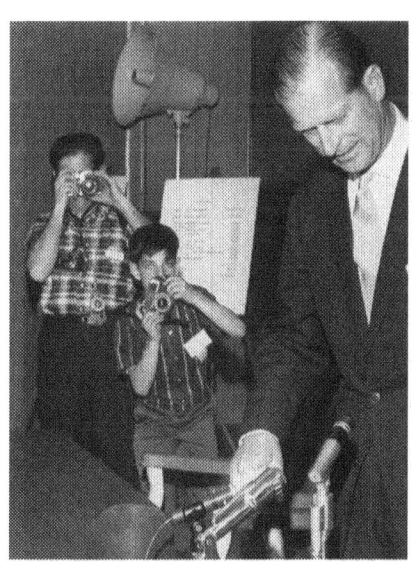

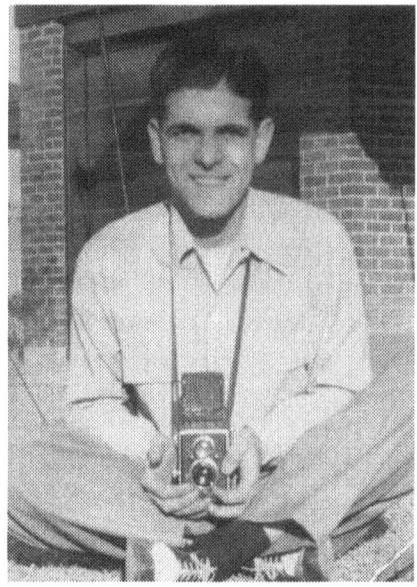

13

Jack Ingram, my copy boy friend at the Herald, was leaving the paper to attend college. I decided that I would go as well. If I wanted to advance in my field I needed a college degree. Jack opted for a junior college the first two years, after which he planned to go to the University of Texas and become a lawyer. As for me, I wanted a BA in Journalism.

We both enrolled in North Texas Junior Agricultural College in Arlington for the spring Semester. This institution became Arlington State during our sophomore year there, and today is known as University of Texas at Arlington.

The week after I quit the Herald, before the start of the spring semester, I decided to take a vacation. I drove east, through Arkansas and Missouri to the Ozarks, where I booked a week's stay at Lake Taneycomo. It was a luxury time at a luxury hotel, and it just about depleted my bank account. My thirty-five dollars a week at the paper had not really covered somewhat extravagant living expenses.

When I arrived in Arlington I was broke. As a result I was forced to look for a job. I found not one, but five.

At school I became editor of the Shorthorn, the college paper. That paid $50 a month. I was the statistician for the Southwest Junior College football conference. That paid $50. I worked two nights and weekends as assistant to a livestock photographer. That paid about $50. I became the part-time correspondent for the Dallas Times Herald and the Fort Worth Press. They paid by the column inch, and together that came to around $50 a month. And finally, dinnertime I waited tables at Macs Coffee shop, where I ate free. If you think all this left little time for study, you are right.

I did have an advantage over other freshmen. For one thing I was older. For another, in 1948, the last year at an English high school was about the equivalent to the first year at an American junior college. Also I took easy courses. For example, I took German for my language requirement. My hardest course was advanced math. The teacher, Sue Boyer, was a fairly attractive dishwater blonde, so I dated her. Even so, I barely made a C plus. Journalism 101 I could have taught myself. Actually I was not interested in grades, as long as I passed the required courses, and my grade point average was high enough for an eventual transfer to a four-year school.

It was in the second semester of my journalism class that I met my future wife, though given the circumstances, no one would have predicted our ever getting together for as much as a date.

She sat one row behind me. The first thing I ever said to her was: "Your lipstick doesn't match your nail polish." Her name was Vivian Luther and her reaction was predictable.

'Who is that conceited fool, and whatever does he think he has to make him that conceited?" Those were her thoughts, she told me later.

Vivian was beautiful. Well proportioned, with azure-blue eyes and long dark hair, she had an air about her that was at once friendly and yet mysterious. When she cut her hair short and wore it in bangs a few years after we met, she could have doubled for Leslie Caron, the French movie star of "An American in Paris."

No matter how much Vivian disliked me, she could not avoid me. I was her editor on the Shorthorn staff. Outside class she tried. There were two campus eateries, one called the Shorthorn, like the paper, the other called the Hut. I ate lunch at the Shorthorn. Vivian hung with the Hut crowd, a bunch of cowboy campus rebels, who deemed us ego-inflated jerks.

Even with my multiple jobs, money was tight. The cheapest item on the Shorthorn menu was their grilled cheese sandwich. That's what I had for lunch almost every day I ate there. Believe it or not, that is still my favorite sandwich.

As the semester progressed, I did try to start up a friendship with Vivian. My chances were diminished when Vivian's gossipy club sisters told her I was going steady with a townie, a local student not living in the dorm.

Hazel Satterwhite lived with her grandmother in Arlington. She and I played a few games of tennis on occasion, after which we showered together. We may have kissed at that point, but any subsequent attempts on my part to engage in sex resulted in Hazel getting hysterical. I was not about to risk being accused of attempted rape. As a green-card alien, I faced deportation if found wanting in the moral turpitude department.

Hazel and I were definitely not going steady. I tried to explain that to Vivian one beautiful spring afternoon. We were sitting on the grass outside the journalism building. My pleadings and protestations, begging her to reconsider our relationship, were becoming tearful. Luckily, before my hay fever attack turned into asthma she took pity on me. I thought it might have been the tears but she told me later that she had never seen anyone have as bad an allergy attack.

That summer I returned to England for a visit with my family. I told Vivian I would write her. I also told her, in my typical foot-in-mouth fashion, that if she lost ten pounds I would marry her. It was intended as a joke. She did not take it as such. It made her so mad she rushed out and devoured a double banana split.

My mother paid for passage on the Queen Mary. I certainly could not have afforded it, though I upgraded it from tourist to cabin class. In keeping with the social status cabin class implied, I bought an expensive white dinner jacket. Other than on the return trip aboard the Mauritania, I never wore it again.

Aboard the voyage from New York to Dover, according to the passenger manifest, was famed playwright Noel Coward, traveling first class of course. As it happened, one of my shipmates sitting at my assigned table, was a young actress from Lake Charles, Louisiana. She had just closed a successful run of Coward's smash hit Blythe Spirit. When she found out that Coward was aboard she desperately wanted to meet him.

Access to First Class from Cabin was strictly limited and by invitation only. I had a better chance than most since I carried press credentials.

"I'll do my best, Charmaine," I told the actress, whose name was Charmaine Thompson, "but I can't promise."

Actually it was a lot easier than I thought. At lunch the next day I asked one of the stewards to take a note to Mr. Coward explaining that I was a journalist interested in a short interview. I also mentioned that my companion, a young actress who had just completed a run of one of his plays, was dying to meet him.

Before we finished lunch I had an answer. Come to see him in his cabin at three o'clock that afternoon, his note said.

Almost beside herself with joy, Charmaine grabbed me around the neck and planted a juicy kiss smack on my lips. I'm sure some of our fellow passengers thought we were honeymooners.

Promptly at three we arrived at Noel Coward's cabin. Charmaine knocked on the door and entered a few steps ahead of me. The great man was reclined on his bunk, his head resting on two plump pillows, dressed only in his skivvies. He was smoking a cigarette in a long holder held between his thumb and forefinger, reading a copy of The Illustrated London News.

It did not seem to bother Mr. Coward to let Charmaine see him in this state of undress, but he quickly covered up with a sheet when I walked in.

"Oh Mr. Coward," Charmaine gushed, "this is such a thrill for me. I'm Charmaine Thompson and I know all your plays."

"It's too big, the Atlantic, isn't it?" Coward intoned with a melodramatic flair.

"Far too big," Charmaine replied, equally theatrical.

"And too deep."

"Much, much too deep."

"I don't care a bit, do you?"

"Not a scrap."

"Excuse me," I interrupted, "but am I missing something here?"

"The opening lines from part 2, scene 5, of Cavalcade," Charmaine explained triumphantly, "except that Mr. Coward was doing the female and I the male parts. Those are he ill-fated honeymooners, Edith and Edward, aboard the Titanic."

"Bravo, old girl," Coward applauded, "that was smashing. By Jove, you do know my plays."

Somehow I never got around to the interview. Those two were having too much fun. We got out of there an hour later.

Charmaine's gratitude for having arranged the meeting knew no bounds. After dinner that evening we strolled the promenade deck feeling romantic. The ocean was calm, a slight breeze ruffled her hair and a huge moon set on the horizon. The scene was almost a cliche. We stopped to embrace and kissed passionately.

"Charmaine, darling," I said, "you know this is just a shipboard romance. Well probably never see each other again."

"I don't care sweetheart," she said, clinging to me, "lets make the most of it. I want to spend the night with you."

There was one minor problem.

Both she and I had cabin mates. I had actually talked to a steward about the possibility of finding us an empty cabin.

"There are no empty cabins, sir, not until tomorrow night," I was told. "After we land at LeHavre several passengers are leaving. Then I will be able to get you into B-204. That's just across from your cabin, sir."

I thanked him and gave him a hefty tip.

It was on the last night of our journey, as the Queen Mary was slowly crossing the English Channel, that Charmaine and I made love.

We never met again after that. But I did see her again, at least I am 99 per-cent sure I did, on the big screen. Her name had been changed, her hair was different, she had lost at least twenty pounds, but that was Charmaine alright, the Hollywood version. If she had looked like that on the Queen Mary I would have proposed.

14

When I first came to school in Arlington, I lived on a chicken ranch, where the Kikers gave me room and some board in exchange for chores. I had to clean out the chicken cages, gather eggs, and handle some odd tasks, like the time a skunk got in with the chickens.

"You have to kill that skunk," old man Kiker told me as he handed me a shotgun. "My eyesight ain't that good anymore. Here, put these on," he said, tossing me a pair of old overalls, "just in case. Get as close as you can, I don't want you to miss and kill any chickens. That damned skunk already got three!"

"Just in case of what?" I asked, never having dealt with a skunk before.

"Never you mind, just go out and do it."

I left through the kitchen door as my landlord watched me through the window. Approaching the cages gingerly, Mr. Kiker motioned me from behind the door to get ever closer.

I could see the skunk in the left corner of the first cage. As I got about ten feet away, it turned its back on me and raised its tail. At this point I had a clear shot and pulled the trigger, but just before I did, I got sprayed. That skunk got me good. I may have killed it, but lord almighty, what a horrible stench. It almost made me pass out.

Inside the kitchen Mr. Kiker was laughing his head off.

"Strip down to your shorts," he yelled through the closed door, "we gotta burn them clothes."

He disappeared from view for a second then came back with a large can of tomato juice.

"This is the only thing that'll kill the smell," he said, as he poured the contents over me while holding his nose. "Sorry, but nothing will ever get the smell outa them things. That's why the overalls."

I could cheerfully have strangled him.

My roommate at the Kikers was Bob Weaver, a young petroleum engineering student, who planned to get his degree from Texas A&M after finishing at Arlington. Since I was the one with a car, if you can call it that, we rode back and forth to school, with Bob sharing the cost of gas. Bob worked the summer as a bellhop at a large Fort Worth hotel.

He told me he made pretty good money in tips, especially from traveling sales-men looking for a little entertainment.

"You mean to tell me you were a pimp?" I teased.

"I certainly was not," he protested, "I was a facilitator. All I ever did was give out a couple of phone numbers."

"You want to give me one?" I said, only halfway jokingly.

"You couldn't afford those women," Bob said. "Besides, if I hadn't done it, the other guys would. I needed the money for college."

That I could understand. And he was right about what I could and couldn't afford. When I did occasionally feel a need for relief, I visited a small establish-ment in North Fort Worth, an area known for such activities. Here Edna, who specialized in college kids, charged me two bucks. She always gave me a good time. She also gave me a dose of crabs.

Most assignments handled by my part-time photographer boss involved valuable Hereford bulls, whose pictures ran in cattle-breeders catalogues. What prospec-tive buyers looked for in an animal was a straight back and enormous testicles. That's really the best way I can describe it.

Some weekends I accompanied Bob Winnegar, one of the Southwest's best live-stock photographers, on photo shoots. We would dig a shallow trench about two feet wide and six to eight inches deep and fill it with straw. Then we would lead the bull into the depression, which made him appear closer to the ground.

The resulting photograph made it appear that the bull's macho machinery hung really low. Ergo, the lower the balls, the higher the stud fee.

It was an accepted practice, as was the retouch job Winnegar did on the bull's back. These animals had pedigrees that would make a Westminster dog show champion look like a mutt. A thoroughbred Hereford bull might be worth over fifty thousand dollars, and that was back in 1948.

Purloining a reject print of one of those animals, I created a Christmas card for myself that offended just about everyone. I superimposed my face on that of the bull, one eye winking salaciously, with the message reading Have a very Merry Christmas, and that's no bull!

To my mother that only re-enforced her theory that America, but especially Texas, had turned me into a boorish, culture lacking, crude cowboy. But that's just my mother. Had I gotten a Harvard Ph.D. in literature she still wouldn't have been satisfied.

During my second semester at Arlington I moved into a private boarding house, run by a Mrs. Swan, mostly for veterans. I was glad to get away from the chickens, but I missed Bob who transferred to Texas A&M.

Vivian, who by now was a little more receptive to my company, was living in the girls dorm. Some days I would drive her back and forth to her home in Dallas. On one of those trips coming back to school, my front right wheel kept on going straight as I turned a corner. We both stared in disbelief, thinking at first it was some other car's. I yelled at Vivian to lean over as close as she could toward me, keeping the car level. I managed to guide it toward the gutter where it came to a stop, brake drum resting on the curb.

The lug nuts had come loose. Luckily I located three of the four on the street behind us and was able to put the wheel back. Vivian assured me that if her father ever found out about this matter, he would ban me from her life. Her dad was a stickler for car maintenance.

Timmy, as we nicknamed the car, had other problems. For one thing, it was hard to start on cold mornings. I would sit there, turning the ignition on and off, stomping on the gas, cussing a blue streak.

Vivian would come along, poke her head through the window, and admonish me for my swearing.

"That's no way to talk to Timmy," she would say in a soothing tone, "you have to talk nice to it."

"Oh yea?" I would argue, "you try it."

Vivian would then replace me in the driver's seat, speak a few words of encouragement to the car, like, "now be a good little Timmy, we love you, please start for me," turn the ignition key, and presto, the car would start. I swear that happened on more than a few occasions. I could never figure it out.

When I returned from England that summer aboard the Mauritania, I made friends with a young Texan who had just spent two years in Saudi Arabia, working as an oil exploration engineer.

Jimmy Jones, from Floydada, Texas, told me he had lived without alcohol or women during that period, and was more than ready to make up for lost time. Since neither one of us was due back before the end of September,—I at school, he at work—we decided to drive to Texas from New York. To that purpose he bought a used car, something he had planned on doing anyway. I would share the cost of gas and maintenance. Along the way we were hoping for a little excitement.

Since neither one of us had been to the country's Capitol, Washington D.C. became our first stop.

We checked into the Senator Hotel, a structure built like an E, with a wing on each side, and one in the middle. The view from our bedroom was toward the rooms of the middle wing. We were lucky to find a room. Apparently there was a big teachers convention being held in town.

After we took showers and cleaned up from the long drive, we were relaxing on our beds when Jimmy happened to glance out his window.

"Shit Fred," he gasped, "look at that! One floor down almost straight across."

I raised up to see what he was staring at but couldn't see across to the floor below. His bed, closer to the window, was obstructing my view.

Jimmy grabbed hold of my arm and dragged me to a spot from which I could see more clearly.

In full view, with the curtains wide open, a young girl was undressing.

"That broad is trolling for company," Jimmy pronounced gleefully. "We gotta get her room number. Quick old buddy, go one floor down and see if you can figure it out."

"You go, old buddy, and I'll stay and watch."

"I saw her first. If we make contact I'll see if she has a room mate."

I couldn't argue with that logic, so I did go to the floor below.

There were three possible rooms, each one of which could be the one matching our window 'exposuree'. Rooms number 253, 255, and 257.

On a hunch, when I returned to our room, Jimmy dialed the middle number. He struck pay dirt. Never, in my entire life, have I heard the line of bullshit my travel companion laid on the young lady that afternoon.

Going along with the teacher convention theme, Jimmy, using an assumed name, convinced her that he was a teacher from, God knows where, I forget the exact details, and that a fellow conventioneer had given him her room number.

He wrote it down, together with her name, he told her, but lost the slip of paper and could remember only the number. As improbable as that all sounds, Jimmy persuaded her to meet him for cocktails in the bar around six.

After she hung up, what happened next had both of us in a state of horny antici-pation bringing sweat to our brows. Totally nude, she flopped onto her bed and inserted what we could only presume to be a contraceptive suppository.

"My gawd Almighty," Jimmy crowed, "DID YOU SEE THAT? "She wants to get laid!"

"Don't we all?" I said. "Now listen Jimmy, you make sure she has a friend. We'll take em to dinner, OK? If she doesn't have one, be sure to bring her up here. We'll share, you hear me? Don't let me down. Promise you'll get her up here. You may' have seen her first but I got the room number.

"I promise," Jimmy assured me.

He must have had his fingers crossed. I waited until eight o'clock. Then I went downstairs to eat dinner. Nothing tasted good.

Back in the room, I fell asleep around midnight watching television. I was awak-ened by the sound of the telephone ringing. I didn't know how long it had rung. Still groggy, I picked it up. It was Jimmy on the other end.

"Where in the hell are you?" I managed to blurt out.

"Fred, you got to help me! I'm in a heap of trouble." He sounded scared.

"Where are you?" I repeated

"I'm at the police station at 4th and F."

"Did you say police station?"

"Yes, they don't believe my name in Jim Jones."

"Show them your drivers license."

"I don't got it, I left my wallet in the room. That's what I want you to bring me, please, Fred, please."

"I should let you stay in jail overnight, you son-of-a-bitch!" I said it, but I didn't mean it. "Would you please tell me what happened?"

"Its a long story, I'll tell you all about it when you bring me my wallet."

I pulled on my clothes, found Jimmy's wallet in his nightstand drawer and took a cab to the police station. He was in a holding cell when I arrived there. I asked to speak to the watch commander. After he checked Jim's ID he asked me to wait. Ten minutes later a chastised looking Jimmy Jones appeared.

"I'll let you go this time," the watch commander told him. "By all rights we should arrest you on an indecent exposure count. Next time get a room. They rent them to tourists, you know?"

In the cab back to the Hotel Jimmy told me his story. He had taken the girl to dinner fully intending to bring her back up the room later. Or so he claimed. The reason he left his wallet in the room was because he did not want to get robbed, in case the girl turned out to be a pro.

Since it was a balmy summer night they decided to take a stroll in LaFayette Park.

"One thing led to another," he tried to explain, "so we laid down in the grass. Then nature took over."

"What's the matter with a comfortable bed, you idiot?" I was getting mad.

"All of a sudden this fucking cop shows up from out of nowhere and plants his foot square on my ass."

"The cop wasn't fucking, you were! Then what happened?"

"He asked for my ID, which I didn't have. The girl had hers in her purse. He asked her if what we were engaged in was consensual, and when she said yes, he let her go."

"Of all the places to expose your dick you had to choose LaFayette Park!"

"I know, I feel so stupid."

"Stupid ain't the word. You're a fucking moron!"

We left Washington two days after the incident. During that time we did get in some sightseeing.

Three years later I was covering an Eisenhower presidential campaign rally for the *Lubbock Avalanche Journal*, my employer at the time.

The rally was held at the Lubbock airport. As I drove back to the paper, a black Mercedes passed me, honking furiously, the driver waving his arm at me.

It was Jimmy Jones.

Jimmy indicated that he would pull over to the side of the road, wanting me to do the same. He speeded up to get a few car lengths ahead of me, then stopped. I pulled up to about three car-lengths behind him.

Almost before the Mercedes came to a halt, Jimmy came bounding out from the driver's side and sprinted toward me.

I rolled down my window.

"Don't mention D.C.!" he gasped, breathing hard, "that's my wife I'm with!"

Since both of us lived in Lubbock, we met on a few other occasions, each time with Jimmy trying to sell me life insurance. That got stale pretty fast. The last time he tried it, I told him that if he mentioned life insurance one more time, I'd tell his wife about D.C.

15

During the summer of '49, while vacationing with my family in London, I wrote a couple of letters to Vivian, mostly chitchat, but also telling her how much I wanted to see her again. Jimmy Jones drove us back to Texas, where Vivian had taken a summer job with the Wall Street Journal. I fully expected to surprise her at work once I got to Dallas, but as it turned out, the surprise was on me.

When I called her home, her mother told me that she was in the hospital after emergency surgery for appendicitis.

"Can she have visitors?" I asked

"Yes, but not for long, she is still pretty weak," her mother said, "maybe tomorrow afternoon."

The next day I bought a dozen red roses and went to see her. Almost all of Vivian's close relatives were there, her mother Louise, father Guy, her two sisters Norma and Jane, and a couple of friends. Louise shooed them all out of the room when I arrived.

"She really likes this one," she told them as I found out later.

Her illness and subsequent operation had caused Vivian to lose ten pounds.

"I thought I said five pounds," I kidded, "you really didn't have to go to this length. I guess I have to marry you now."

Vivian did not think that was very funny.

One morning, while still in the hospital recuperating, Vivian was sitting in her wheelchair in the hallway while her room was being made up. Sitting in another wheelchair was a young man who had also been operated on for appendicitis. The two struck up a conversation. Having similar operations was not the only coincidence. The young man had also been a student at Arlington State when it was still NTJAC, but before Vivian got there. Now he was attending Texas A&M. Would she agree to go out with him once each got well?

That semester her family doctor would not allow Vivian to go back to school. Living in the dorm and attending classes meant climbing stairs, and Dr. Shuett did not think she was strong enough for that. The Wall Street Journal had kept her on, so as soon as she was able, Vivian returned to work.

The only day I could come to Dallas from school was Sundays. It was also the only day I enjoyed a home-cooked meal. Vivian's mother Louise made the absolutely best fried chicken I have ever tasted.

For our first date, I took Vivian to see 'One Touch of Venus', starring Ava Gardner. The movie was showing at the Texas Theater on Jefferson Boulevard in Dallas, the same theater where Kennedy assassin Lee Harvey Oswald was captured fourteen years later.

Leaving the theater balcony after the show, I tripped on the first step of the plush, red-carpeted, winding staircase, and tumbled, in what appeared to be slow motion, head over heels all the way down to the bottom. Vivian followed behind, unable to suppress her almost hysterical laughter.

Arriving at the foot of the stairs, I got up as though nothing had happened, and without missing a beat, I turned to her and said: "You see, I told you I was falling for you!"

I might have been the one she really liked, but that didn't stop Vivian from dating her new friend from Baylor Hospital. She was honest with him though. She told him that Sundays were reserved for somebody else. Who that somebody was she would not tell him. Neither would she tell me who her other beau was. But sometimes truth is indeed stranger than fiction.

Out of curiosity, and perhaps out of jealousy, the other man in Vivian's life drove past her house one Sunday and discovered who I was. Parked outside was a car he recognized. It was a car he had ridden in many times. Robert Weaver, my roommate at the Kikers chicken ranch was Vivian's other man.

The biggest social event at Texas A&M is the annual homecoming game when the opposing team is the University of Texas. When an Aggie asks his date to join him for that homecoming weekend, it is tantamount to a proposal.

Bob Weaver asked Vivian to come to College Station for THE BIG WEEKEND in the fall of 1949. She thought about it, realizing that a yes might be misconstrued. She liked Bob, had in fact met his parents, but had never seriously considered marriage.

The weekend before the big game Vivian dated Bob one last time. She explained that she was very fond of him but that she really did not love him enough to consider marriage.

With me, on the other hand, marriage was a distinct possibility.

I like to tell people that Bob and I fought for Vivian's affections. It was a fight to the finish, I'd tell them, and I lost. I ended up marrying her.

That was another thing Vivian didn't think was very funny. But then I spent my life making jokes. Mostly they went unappreciated. I guess that should have told me something.

By the spring semester Vivian was well enough to come back to school. Instead of living in the dorm, she chose to live in a private residence for coeds run by a Mrs. Cox. The house that I lived in, Swan House, was just a half block from Cox House. Mrs. Cox did not allow male visitors anywhere except the front parlor. No wonder! Vivian told me one of her roommates ran around stark naked. I always thought the boys should have hung out at Cox house. I know, bad pun! That's the only kind I make.

Timmy, my faded black '36 Chevvy, was always parked in front of Swan house when I wasn't driving it. Among other things that needed fixing, the seatback was loose. Sometimes it would lean back a few inches more on one side than the other. That gave me an idea. Why not have it go all the way down, opening a large space into the trunk? That way one could crawl from the front into the trunk, stretch out and go to sleep. Useful on long trips, right? Naturally I would have to fix it so that it maintained its upright position while the car was being driven. Vivian actually helped me with the mechanics. Her dad had taught her how to use tools.

Now Timmy boasted a reclining seat. I understand that these days many cars are designed with reclining front seats. I should have patented the idea. Actually sleeping in the trunk on long trips was the last thing on my mind.

One evening, coming back from a date with Vivian, I parked the car on a campus dirt road, a fairly secluded spot not visited often by security patrols. With the seat fully reclined, we got into some serious petting, stripping off bits of clothing one by one. Eventually we were hugging, heads on the seatback, bodies in the trunk going about as far as one can without actual intercourse.

By mutual consent, and because I respected Vivian's high morals, having sex was taboo before marriage.

In retrospect, thinking about having sex with Vivian at that time brings up an ironic image. It had not been too many weeks since my unfortunate encounter with Edna's body lice in that Fort Worth bordello. Curing crabs in those days entailed shaving off all your lower body hair, especially around the pubis. The stubble growing back slowly was evolving into bristles.

Vivian, at about the same time, had had her emergency appendectomy, which in turn necessitated shaving off all the hair in her pubic area. It too was now growing back slowly. Had we made love then we might have stuck together like Velcro. I can't imagine two hedgehogs having a more difficult time.

We both heard it, the sound of a car engine. That could mean only one thing: The Cops! We were going to get busted. All I could think of was pulling a blanket over our heads and staying motionless. Someone shone a flashlight through the windshield. They moved around to the driver side and flashed a light there. Then came the sound of footsteps retreating through gravel. Finally silence!

To this day I still can not figure out if the cop saw us and had pity or didn't see us and left. Whenever Vivian and I talked about that night we shuddered at the recollection. What if, we asked rhetorically? How could we have been so stupid? How could we have taken such a chance? You may only be young once, but that night we each aged at least ten years.

16

After Vivian turned down Bob Weaver's invitation, I was determined not to face a similar rejection.

Late one night at her house, as we were enjoying the warmth of an open fire and listening to KIXL, Dallas' easy listening station, I proposed marriage for the umpteenth time.

"You're just saying that, you don't really mean it," Vivian argued. "You'll never marry me!"

"Yes I will!" I protested. "Lets set a date right here and now. What about a June wedding?"

That's how June 3rd, 1950, became the target date for our nuptials.

Vivian did not want a large wedding and I did not want to get married in a church.

"Darling, if you want to get married in a synagogue, maybe you would like me to convert to Judaism?" Vivian offered.

"I don't and I don't," I said, "if I wanted to marry a Jewish Princess I could have stayed in England. Why can't we have a ceremony that does not mention Jesus, but still invokes a higher presence?

Our campus chaplain was the Rev. Dickey, a Presbyterian. We asked him if he would perform such a service and he agreed. When we told Vivian's parents of our plans, her mother insisted we get married at their house. That we were more than happy to do.

But now came the hard part, telling my family.

To hear my mother tell it, nobody in our family had ever married outside the faith. That wasn't altogether true. Eri's brother Bertie, younger son of Martha Jacoby, my aunt with the Brighton boarding house, married Winifred, a gentile. I am not sure whether she ever converted. I do know that she attended temple on some high holidays, but that didn't stop Martha's Jewish friends from ungallantly referring to her as Bertie's schicksa. Of course they did it behind her back.

Eri himself, for years, had an affair with his non-Jewish secretary, but waited until his mother died before he married her.

Now I was going to bring another schicksa into the family.

"Jews marry Jews," my mother said, "let the gentiles intermarry among their various denominations."

"I don't care how much you love her or how much she loves you," my mother warned, "the day will come when the two of you have a fight and she'll call you a 'Dirty Jew' or worse.

"So what," I countered "then I'll call her a dirty shicksa."

Vivian's mother wrote my family to invite them to the wedding, but neither my mother nor my sister agreed to come. My sister simply ignored the invitation and my mother pleaded ill health.

There followed letters and phone calls begging me not to go through with it. Then the shit hit the proverbial fan.

My sister Lili sent me a telegram, which stated simply that if I married this woman my mother would commit suicide. I can't remember for sure, but I believe she even had the gall to address it to Vivian's home.

That did it. If she thought the telegram would make me hesitate, it had just the opposite effect.

Despite the fact that our formal wedding was scheduled for the 3rd of June, I persuaded Vivian to elope with me the following weekend.

"That way I don't give a damn what my folks think or do," I explained, "it will be a fait accompli, and nobody will be able to do a thing about it."

"What will we tell my mother?" Vivian demurred, "she is looking forward to the wedding."

"We just won't tell her! We simply won't tell anybody! It'll be our little secret. And we'll go ahead with the June wedding as planned."

It took some persuading, but in the end Vivian agreed.

We went to a public clinic to get our blood tests, knowing full well that in order to keep our secret, we would have to take another before June. Vivian always claimed that's what convinced her that I really loved her. She knew how scared as I was of needles.

Rockwall, Texas is a Marriage Mill a short drive north of Dallas where the Justice of the Peace earns a pretty penny, performing weddings on demand. No fuss, no muss, no waiting! All one needed was the blood test certificate and a wedding license form.

On Saturday, April 15, 1950, Vivian and I drove to Rockwall, where the J.P. married us with his wife as witness. I believe there were three other couples ahead of us. At the conclusion of the short ceremony, we were walking down the steps of the courthouse when Mrs. Justice came running after us.

"Haven't you forgotten something?" she asked a little sheepishly.

I had forgotten to pay the poor man, and the wife was not about to let me get away with it. Apologizing profusely I handed over a five-dollar bill.

"What a way to start our marriage, you deadbeat," my brand new wife chided. Actually we had a good laugh over it.

April 15th happens to be my birthday. I picked that date so I would never forget our wedding anniversary. How was I to know that date would also become the deadline for sending in your income tax returns. Wedding anniversary, birthday, and tax deadline, what a trifecta!

That evening, to celebrate, we drove to a fancy Italian restaurant where they only had Valet Parking. My beat up old Chevvy must have looked grossly out of place among the Mercedes, Cadillacs and Lincolns, but I told Timmy he was as good as any car and to hold his hood up high. I really did that!

Vivian had taught me to talk to inanimate objects and I didn't even feel silly about it. Hey, whatever works!

We enjoyed a fine meal, but after paying the check I realized we had a minor problem. Vivian wanted to go dancing, in which case we would have no money left for a hotel. Having waited this long to consummate our relationship I was willing to wait another day. I left the decision up to Vivian.

We spent the night at the Colonial Motel.

Sunday afternoon Vivian's mother arranged a small birthday celebration in my honor. As it happened, Alice Steves, the daughter of the Luthers' neighbors, was also celebrating her birthday and was invited to the party. The birthday cake decoration read 'Fred and Alice'. I get a kick out of telling people that Vivian's wedding cake had another woman's name on it.

Now we were officially married but living apart. Between the night at the Colonial Motel and our June wedding, we only had sex once. That was at a small motel on the Fort Worth to Arlington highway, far enough away where we hoped we would not get spotted.

It was shortly before finals, and between the sex and the studying, we got very little sleep.

In the morning I barely managed to drive Vivian back to school in time for Norton McGiffin's eight o'clock history class. When I saw her coming out of McGiffin's room after class her face was flushed and she looked close to tears.

"What on earth is the matter?" I asked

"I fell asleep during Norton's class," she whispered. "When the bell woke me up Norton looked straight at me and said may I suggest Miss Luther, that you have Fred wake you up a little sooner in the mornings." She began to cry.

"Oh God, I'm so embarrassed. He must have seen us coming out of the motel. You know he lives in Fort Worth. That's just about the time he would drive by."

"So what, you don't know that," I said trying to calm her down.

"Everybody recognizes your car, I'm sure that's what happened." She got agitated again. "Norton doesn't know were married, he must think I'm some sort of slut."

"Oh come one, you're blowing this way out of proportion. Norton knows we're an item. Besides, he's a pretty sophisticated individual, he was probably just trying to be nice."

"I'm crazy about that man, "Vivian said, slightly more calm now. "I don't want him to get the wrong impression."

"That's not going to happen. I'm sure you are one of his favorite students. Now, if he asks you to go to a motel with him, well now, that's a whole different ball-game."

"Shut up, that's not funny." Vivian was mad. "Why do you always have to make a joke out of everything?"

17

Our June 3rd wedding at the Luther home was all we could have asked for. Jack Ingram, my copyboy friend from Denison was best man, the Rev. Dickey conducted the simple ceremony without invoking the name of Christ, and this time our small wedding cake did not have some other woman's name on it.

Jack drove us to the train station for our three-day honeymoon in Galveston, and Vivian's mom decided to use that time to completely clean house, especially Vivian's bedroom, where we would stay for the next few weeks.

Other than the fact that our room at the old Hotel Galveston was right next door to a twenty-four hour remodeling project, that we heard hammering throughout the night, that I got a very nasty sunburn all over my chest, and that I spent money we could not afford in some beachfront gambling joint, we did have a glorious time.

On the early morning train ride back to Dallas we went to the dining car for breakfast. I asked Vivian if she had any money on her, but she did not. Counting all my folding money and coin, I had about a buck seventy-five. This was the days before credit cards.

Vivian was very accommodating.

"Don't worry honey, I'll just have coffee," she volunteered.

What followed was like a scene out of an Abbott and Costello movie. When the waiter showed up to take our order she asked for coffee.

"Are you sure you don't want anything to eat, maybe a boiled egg?" I offered.

"No, I'm not hungry, just coffee."

"How about some toast, surely could can eat a slice of toast?

"Really, darling, coffee will be fine."

"Okay then," I told the waiter, "my wife will have a cup of coffee, and I'll have two eggs over easy, sausage, white toast and tea."

I wish I had a picture of the look on my bride's face that early morning on the train to Dallas. It spoke volumes.

Arriving back that evening at Vivian's home, we were met by her mother. She was sitting on the front porch looking a little strange.

"What's the matter, mother?" Vivian asked. "You're sitting there with that little chicken look on your face. Is something wrong?"

"Why didn't you tell me?" Louise asked in a hurt tone.

"Tell you what, mother?"

But we knew what this was all about.

To insure that our elopement remain secret, we had to make certain that no one would see our Rockwall marriage license. We did not want to take it along, so Vivian got the brilliant idea to hide it behind a picture frame on a wall of her room. It was an autographed picture of Larry Tierney, an actor to whom her California aunt had once rented a room.

"I didn't think you'd want the photo of another man on the wall," her mother explained, "so I took it down. When I cleaned the frame I saw the license. You could have told me."

"I'm sorry mother, I knew you had planned our wedding and I didn't want to disappoint you. I'll tell you why we did it."

Vivian explained our reason for getting married.

"Don't worry, mom, I'm not pregnant. It was Fred's sister. Her telegram did it. Fred insisted we get married right away. That way, he said, there was nothing any one could do about it."

"You can never tell your father," Louise warned. "No telling what he'd do."

Vivian's father, Guy 'Pappy' Luther, worked as a projectionist in Dallas movie theaters. Louise always called him Luther. He was active in IATSE union affairs, holding different offices at various times. It was his idea to teach me the profession.

"It may help you pay your way through college," he said. "I can probably get you a job in a Denton Drive In theater."

The next few weeks I spent my evenings in the projection booth of the Melrose Theater in downtown Dallas. Pappy was a good teacher. It helped that he was fond of me. Vivian was his favorite. He called her cowboy. The youngest of three daughters, she was definitely daddy's girl and probably understood him better than anyone. He was subject to moody periods when he would sit around, sucking on his pipe, not saying a word. I often wondered what he thought about a German Jewish kid marrying the apple of his eye.

Vivian told me that of his three sons-in-law he liked me the best. Without Pappy Luther I would never have made it through college.

In the fall of 1950, Vivian and I both enrolled in North Texas State at Denton. We moved into a small box of a garage apartment within walking distance of school. The apartment gave the appearance of having been built by a man with a physical problem, as in deed it had. The owner's left leg was shorter than his right. I know it sounds a little cruel and unkind to say this, but I swear the entire apartment, including the staircase, leaned to the left. Apart from that, our landlords, Mr. and Mrs. Lamb were the nicest people. Mrs. Lamb often brought us home baked pies and other goodies.

Pappy Luther did manage to get me a temporary union card and with it the projectionist job at the Denton Drive In. I did not make union wages since the job came with certain limitations. The owner was old man Franklin with his wife Jo, a part Indian, who actually helped pour the concrete when some of the speaker poles needed replacing. When she wore knee-length skirts or shorts you could see dried cement stuck to the hairs on her legs.

The old man was a mean son of a bitch. There simply is no other way to say it. When I complained about the fist-sized tarantulas infesting the projection booth dugout, he called me a sissy and told me to ignore the critters. The old man had a terrible case of spondylitis, which caused his shoulders to stoop, and his head to be permanently bent over. That's probably why he was so mean.

For thirty-five dollars a week I spent six nights a week showing B-movies or worse to an audience more interested in what was going on in the back seat of cars than what showed on the screen.

During the long fall and winter months we put on two shows, some even double-features, which meant I would not get out of the place until way after midnight. That's when I became creative.

Film came on reels in cans those days. Some were as long as four reels. For the second showing I would do some personal editing. I might run the third reel to a point where I could cut out several scenes then switch to a part of the last reel where it appeared to make sense. In my Drive In, many faces ended up on the cutting room floor. And I got home a half-hour sooner.

The day before Christmas Eve I was fired. It was not for anything I'd done. Old man Franklin decided he could not make enough money by staying open. The weather was bad, people spent money for things other than entertainment, and I went without a paycheck for three weeks. Finally he called.

"You can come back to work next Friday but I'm cutting your salary to thirty dollars, and by the way, if your wife wants to come she'll have to pay for her ticket like everyone else," he informed me.

What choice did I have? By the time the fall semester came around my wife was five months pregnant. While I was getting my B.A., she was getting her BABY. Our baby, actually.

◆　　　◆　　　◆

From the day I came to this country I began the process of becoming a citizen. Marrying Vivian speeded up the process. She has never let me forget that.

"You only married me so you could become an American," she would tease.

"No, I married you for your money. That and your mother's fried chicken!"

Becoming a citizen is not that easy. In my particular case the Naturalization and Immigration examiner took it upon himself to put me through the ropes. Since I was a college student taking history courses among other subjects, he decided that I needed to know the names of every last president, plus the dates of various American Revolution events. Luckily I was prepared.

Who wasn't prepared was my mother-in-law.

The petitioner for citizenship is not the only person interviewed by the government. Friends and relatives are also questioned as to the qualifications of the applicant. Things like moral turpitude, political affiliations, work habits, or possible criminal background, come into play, as well as various dates and other statistics.

When Louise was called in during my final interrogation, the examiner asked me to leave the room so he could chat privately with her.

"Now Mrs. Luther," he began, "just a few questions, if you don't mind. How long have you known the applicant?"

"I first met him when my daughter was in the hospital in the summer of 1949. I liked him right away."

"Has he ever discussed politics with you?"

"Not really. I'm not a political person."

"Do you happen to know the year and date of his birthday?"

"Yes, of course. April 15, 1925, in Berlin, Germany."

"Now could you tell me the date of his marriage to your daughter Vivian?"

"June 3rd, 1950."

"Did you say June?"

"Yes, June 3rd, at our house."

"Are you sure?"

"Yes, of course I'm sure." Louise was beginning to get nervous. The interview had taken on an ominous tone.

The examiner put the clipboard with his notes on the desk between them.

"Mrs. Luther," he asked sternly, "are you familiar with the term perjury? You are under oath, you know!" He looked at his notes. "June is not the date your son-in-law gave us."

Louise was close to tears.

"Mrs. Luther, let me suggest this to you. I will let you go outside to confer briefly with your son-in-law. Then when you come back in, maybe we can sort this matter out."

When Louise came out of his office she looked worried.

"He wants me to tell him you were married on April 15," she said," but if that is on any document Luther sees he will get very angry. I don't know what to do."

"Louise, darling, you have to tell the truth. Don't worry about Luther. If it comes to that, I'll deal with it. Promise."

"Vivian and Fred were married on April 15th in Rockwall, but they tried to keep it a secret." Louise told the man when she returned for the interview. "I don't recognize that date, as far as I'm concerned it was June."

"Well, that's for your personal peace of mind, Mrs. Luther," the examiner explained, "but you realize as far as the government is concerned, there is only one official date. So I will put down that you said April 15, all right?"

"I suppose so, but my husband does not know. I just hope he doesn't find out."

The day on which I became a citizen was June 23rd 1951. The ceremony was in the courtroom of Judge Thomas Stillwell, a no nonsense jurist with a reputation for strict enforcement of the law.

As luck would have it, Pappy Luther was working early that morning, so Louise's neighbor Mr. Steves agreed to act as one of my ssponsors and drove us to the courthouse. Louise was still worried that the date of our elopement would be made public in the courtroom.

Vivian, Louise and Mr. Steves got to sit in the front row, ready to congratulate me after the ceremony. There were only six of us that day, my case coming up third. Back then individuals were still naturalized on a more or less individual basis, nothing like today's mass procedures when sometimes over a hundred applicants, all waving little American flags, become citizens in one lump.

As part of the ceremony, the judge questions the examiner about the petitioner's qualification for citizenship, and any background information he, the judge, should be made aware of.

The man ahead of me had forty-eight outstanding parking tickets. The judge turned to him and asked if he was ready to pay all tickets in full right there and then.

"I have the check made out, your Honor," he said, proffering it to the bench. "I am sorry. It wont happen again."

"Citizenship brings with it responsibilities," the judge lectured, "and paying your dues certainly includes paying parking fines. Okay, who is next?

"Mr. Fritz Baumann," the bailiff said, "he is asking the court to legally change his name."

"We will get to that in a second," Judge Stillwell intoned, turning to the NIS examiner, "what can you tell me about Mr. Baumann?

"Mr. Baumann was convicted of a smuggling offense in 1947, your Honor," the examiner explained. "Judge Stillwell's ears pricked up and my mother-in-law almost passed out.

Smuggling! That could mean only one thing, cocaine or heroin. Vivian's husband was a dope smuggler!

"Will the petitioner step up to the bench please," the judge ordered.

"Now then, young man, what is this all about?"

I explained the circumstances of the offense to the judge. Unfortunately my cheering section could not hear what was being said. I had never told Vivian or her family about the gloves. They were expecting to hear the worst.

"You may step back," the judge told me. "I want you to start life as an American citizen with a clean slate. I am therefore expunging the record and any reference to this unfortunate incident. Good luck young man, be a proud American."

That my people heard. When I explained the whole situation, Louise actually laughed.

"For a moment I really thought my daughter had made a huge mistake," she confessed. "What happened to the gloves? Did you get to keep any?"

"No, they were all confiscated as evidence. I never saw them again."

18

As the date approached for the birth of our son, Vivian's mother asked her to return to Texas a month ahead of the blessed event. Not only would she be able to look after her properly, the gynecologist would be Dr. Massey, the best Dallas had to offer. He was recommended by the Luther family doctor. To the best of our reckoning, the baby was due on December 31st.

While Vivian was in Dallas, my mother came to visit me in Denton. She was not about to miss the birth of her first grandchild. Now being Jewish was not that important. All was forgiven, especially since my sister had not been able to get pregnant. She tried for years, finally resorting to adoption. Once again her little brother had succeeded where she had not. I am sure that contributed to her sibling jealousy.

Vivian never brought up the subject of the poison pen telegram with my mother, who after I asked her about it, claimed to be unaware Lili had sent it. My mother stayed with us for almost four months. Make all the mother-in-law jokes you want to, the two women managed to get along. They had something in common, both loved me, and both loved the baby. Eventually they became friends. For that my wife, I am convinced, was the driving force. My sister was a different matter. Vivian is part Cherokee. Them mean Indians bear grudges.

Our son, as he would be throughout his entire life, was late. He was born on January 5th, 1952, a Saturday. We named him Guy Caesar, after his two grandfathers.

Early that morning I got a phone call from Louise telling me about the eminent event. Vivian started having labor pains around 5 a.m. she said, and could I make it down to Dallas. Saturday at the Drive In is a big night. Mean old Mr. Franklin told me he didn't care if my wife had triplets.

"If you're not here to open the show don't bother to come back," he warned. I knew he meant it.

My mother had her suitcase packed, and we drove to Dallas that morning. In order for me to get back to Denton on time, Guy had to be born no later than 3 p.m., and that was cutting it thin.

Back then, doctors had Saturday office hours until noon. Hospital visits came later. Dr. Massey, Vivian's obstetrician, ordered a shot to slow down her labor so he could make it to the maternity ward before Guy's arrival.

Baylor's Florence Nightingale maternity clinic is one of the best in the country. But administering a sedative to accommodate a doctor's hours I thought a little odd, especially since I was hoping for a speedy delivery.

Job or no job, I had made up my mind to be there for my son's birth. The hours dragged on. Finally, close to 3 p.m., they wheeled Vivian into the operating room. I had to wait outside. A short while later an orderly pushed a metal cart out of the OR.

"Congratulations, it's a boy," he said, as his cart hit a wheelchair someone had left in the hallway. A tray spilled to the floor right at my feet. I never found out what it was. If it was some of the afterbirth, at least I could never joke that they threw away the baby and kept the afterbirth.

"You have to drive back," both my mother and mother-in-law urged. "It's going to be dark soon."

I stayed just long enough to have a nurse show me my son through the maternity ward window. Never was there a more beautiful baby boy.

Normal drive time from Dallas to Denton, obeying the speed limit, is roughly an hour. That night I made it in thirty-nine minutes.

◆　　　◆　　　◆

My first job out of college was on the Plainview Herald, a small paper in the West Texas Panhandle. My job application requested a starting salary of sixty-five dollars a week. It was a sum nobody thought I could get right out of college, but I did. Perhaps the fact that I had already worked a year at the Denison newspaper made the difference.

When Vivian and I met Mr. Hilburn, the editor and owner of the paper, he assured us that even though it might get hot during the day, we would sleep under a blanket every night. What he failed to mention was that it would be a blanket of sand.

Plainview, Texas, like many other west Texas towns, was suffering a series of dust storms the likes of which had not been seen since the '30s. It was the beginning of a long and costly drought. Luckily the town did not depend on rainfall for its water supply. That came from artesian wells. Other towns and cities west of the Caprock were not that fortunate. Crops were beginning to suffer.

Our apartment was upstairs in a large prairie style bungalow. The downstairs was converted into a duplex, both of which were rented to elderly couples. Their apartments had separate doors. We entered by the main door into a foyer and climbed the staircase of the original dwelling. We did not have an upstairs door. In case of a fire, the stairwell would become a natural flue.

The place was a firetrap. With a five months old baby, Vivian worried day and night. Behind the house was a large oak tree, close enough to climb on, had there been a limb low enough to reach. I thought about buying a rope ladder, but where could you find one in Plainview?

As a compromise I nailed a bunch of short two-by-fours to the trunk, forming an improvised ladder. We had a fire drill, amusing the neighbors who were watching.

Despite its drawbacks, the place had us thrilled at first. But after 5 p.m. we had no water pressure. The old folks downstairs ate dinners early and washed their dishes. Sometimes it would be close to ten p.m. before Vivian could bathe the baby.

On our first night there, the old refrigerator was frozen solid. Vivian had to defrost the thing in order to prepare baby formula. The second night the freezer compartment was frozen solid again. Vivian had to defrost it every night.

One night we woke to choking sounds from Guy. The refrigerator motor had caught fire, sending black smoke into the apartment. It was making the baby choke. I grabbed Guy, and we spent the night sitting on the front porch until morning.

Our time in Plainview was not the happiest of experiences. When an offer came along from the bigger Lubbock Avalanche-Journal, I left the Herald after only five months. I know this had nothing to do with my being hired, but the publisher's name was Charles Guy. His last name was my son's first. Not that I'm superstitious or anything, but I looked upon that as a good omen.

A lot sooner than I could have hoped for, I was working on a fairly large newspaper for seventy-five dollars a week, ten bucks more than at the Herald. There was only one drawback. Since the Avalanche Journal was a morning paper, I had to work nights. That was not all-together bad. Though it meant sleeping in the morning hours, I had enough time during the day to be with my wife and child when other fathers were working.

Some nights after work I did not go directly home. Phil Record, a fellow reporter and bachelor, hosted poker games, nickel and dime stuff, but a lot of fun. Since Lubbock, like Denison, was dry, Phil brewed his own beer. One night, around the witching hour, six of us were sitting in his living room playing cards when there was an explosion that rocked the whole building.

At first we thought a gas main somewhere had blown up. Phil's reaction soon told us what had actually happened.

"God damn it, he yelled," as he jumped up and ran to a closet in his bedroom, "that's a whole week's supply gone to hell!"

A half dozen bottles of home brew had exploded inside the closet. Apparently it wasn't the first time that had happened.

"Sorry fellows," he apologized, "want to help me clean up the mess? We'll finish the game tomorrow."

My job at the Lubbock paper, besides reporting and photography, included some weekend desk duties as an assistant city editor. That included going down to the back-shop where the pages were put together. Technology had not yet changed. Type was still cast on linotype machines and placed in flats, from which mats were rolled to go on the presses.

Late one Saturday, close to deadline, I went downstairs to check on the front-page layout. A headline was on the wrong side of the page, so I picked up the type and moved it to where I had indicated on the makeup sheet.

Suddenly there came three loud blasts from a whistle and work stopped. Then everyone walked out except the shop foreman. I had no idea what happened.

"What is this, a fire drill?" I asked somewhat irritated. "We're close to deadline here!"

"It's a work stoppage, you broke union rules," the foreman explained.

"I did what?"

"You moved some type on the page. Only union members are allowed to do that."

We were not unionized in the newsroom, but the back-shop was. I had indeed broken their rule.

"Oh my God, you know I'm a rookie. Want to get me fired? Please, explain to the men that I had no idea."

Fortunately for me, the foremen called the men back in.

"Just this once," he told me, "let this be a lesson. You don't touch no fucking type, deadline or no deadline, capice?"

Combination reporter/photographer jobs generally don't allow for much advancement. To become really successful in the business you had to specialize. Although I considered my self first and foremost a reporter, I got an eye-opening glimpse into the high paying field of magazine photography when LIFE called.

No telling where or how LIFE got my name. They were looking for a freelance photographer who could cover the ever more damaging drought in West Texas and southern Oklahoma. Farmers, who could no longer count on irrigation wells to water their crops, could not make mortgage payments or cover their bank loans. Many were facing foreclosure.

Choking sandstorms were making life miserable. As depicted in the Depression era novel 'The Grapes of Wrath', people were abandoning their farms, packing up their belongings and heading west.

When the call came from LIFE, I was about to have my two days off, plus a comp day I had earned in lieu of overtime pay. That gave me time for the freelance assignment. LIFE offered me fifty bucks a day plus expenses. For someone making seventy-five dollars a week that was a small fortune.

I spent the next three days roaming the Texas Panhandle and parts of Oklahoma, chronicling the misery and anguish of these down to earth folks. Through no fault of their own, they were facing poverty, and what's worse, the loss of something they and their parents before them had worked so hard to achieve.

On Monday night I drove my take to the Lubbock airport and air-expressed almost three dozen 4x5 negative to New York. Two days later I got a call from an assistant picture editor complimenting me on my efforts.

"Nice work, Fred," he said, "not quite as impressive as Dorothea Lange, but close. Look for your stuff in next weeks issue."

Dorothea Lange was that great depression era photographer whose images of gaunt eyed farmers' wives and starving children became classics. I felt thrilled at the comparison. I could hardly wait to run down to the newsstand the next Tuesday morning to grab a copy of the magazine.

Not one of my pictures had run. The only image used to tell the story was a double-truck aerial photo of a dried up Rio Grande, shot by their ace photographer John Dominis. I didn't know it then, but LIFE had a reputation for throwing money at photographers, paying their travel costs and expense accounts, and then not using their photos.

Something else I didn't know then was that my unused photos would be the impetus for a life-changing career move a few months down the road.

19

By the end of 1953 I had worked for three papers full-time and two part-time, and my current job was giving me enough satisfaction to stick it out for a while.

That Thanksgiving we planned a trip to California to visit Vivian's aunt Marguerite. She was the aunt who had rented a room to Lawrence Tierney, behind whose photo our first marriage license had been unsuccessfully secreted.

A few months earlier I found out that my unused Texas drought photos had been sold to Hearst's International News Service, the wire service ranking third, behind the Associated Press and United Press International. LIFE magazine had a sales department for just such transactions, with the original photographer getting fifty percent of the proceeds.

Charlie Heckman, who was photo chief for INS, had called to compliment me on the take and told me to come see him if I happened to be in Los Angeles. I paid Charlie a courtesy visit, and not just to see how my pictures had been used, but also because it never hurts to make a new contacts.

It came as quite a surprise when Charlie told me there was a job he had recommended me for at the Riverside (CA) Press-Enterprise, an INS subscriber.

"They're looking for a good photographer," he told me, "and I think you just fit the bill."

"But Charlie, I am not looking for a job, and especially not for a photo spot. I like reporting too much."

"Well I don't know how good a writer you are," Charlie said, "but I know you're a hell of a good shooter."

"Where is Riverside?"

"You must have come right through it on your way out here, its half way between Los Angeles and Palm Springs."

"Don't believe so, we came on Route 66, through San Bernardino."

"Okay, well its about ten mile south of there. Let me give them a call and tell them you'll stop by, as a favor to me, Charlie insisted.

"It would have to be on Thanksgiving Day, that's when we are heading home."

Thanksgiving Day of 1953 I stopped by the Riverside paper on our way back to Lubbock. The job indeed was for a photographer, a staff position never before held by anyone. Any photos used by the paper were either wire photos or shot by local commercial photographers.

"What we are looking for is someone to start a photo department from scratch," Howard H Hays Jr.,—the H stood for nothing, hence no period—the editor told me. "Currently we have no darkroom, but within a year we are moving into a new building. You get to design your own. I think we are offering you quite an opportunity."

"How soon would you want me?" I asked, halfway inclined to accept this responsibility.

"As soon as possible, two weeks hopefully."

"I'm sorry Mr. Hays, but that takes me out of consideration. I'm from England, and the least time I would want for giving notice is three months. I'm sorry, but thanks for the offer."

With that I headed out of his office to pick up my wife who had waited at a nearby coffee shop. We were on our way back to Texas.

Arriving back in Lubbock I wrote a letter to Mr. Hays thanking him for giving me the opportunity but formally declining his offer.

On December 1st I received the following telegram:

I WAS SORRY TO GET YOUR LETTER. WE WERE MUCH MORE IMPRESSED WITH YOU THAN WITH ANYONE ELSE WE HAVE TALKED TO AND FEEL THAT YOU WOULD FIT INTO OUR ORGANIZATION EXCEPTIONALLY WELL. IF YOU ARE STILL INTERESTED IN COMING HERE I WISH YOU WOULD ADVISE ME AS TO THE EARLIEST DATE YOU COULD COME. THEN WE WOULD DECIDE WHETHER WE COULD WAIT THAT LONG AND OUR INCLINATION WOULD BE TO WAIT. COULD YOU PHONE ME HERE PERSON TO PERSON COLLECT

It was an offer I could not refuse. What had not been discussed up to this moment was salary. What should I ask for? What dare I ask for?

Vivian and I spent a couple of sleepless nights wondering if I dare ask for a cool hundred a week. That was one third more than the seventy-five I was making in Lubbock. In the end we decided that ninety-five sounded a whole lot better. That's what I asked for and that's what I got. Months later I found out that had I asked for a hundred twenty-five I would have gotten that too.

Once again the Bauman family was on the move, this time to Southern California, a place some people consider the nearest thing to paradise, When he heard that we were going to live in Riverside, Viv's dad did not exactly concur with that description.

"Riverside, that's wino country," he said.

When we arrived in paradise, it was raining cats and dogs. The home Vivian's uncle Walter, Marguerites husband, had rented for us was in a rural slum, and our furniture, what little there was, had not arrived. It was Saturday, Feb. 13th, normally a lucky date for me. My mother was born on a thirteenth.

Uncle Walter had put in a bed but not much else. The stove was an antique dating back to the early thirties. We did not have a television or radio and most lights had 60-watt bulbs. It rained throughout Sunday so what else could we do but go to bed. Little Guy had to sleep on a makeshift pallet of blankets and sleeping bags, but at least he had his basket of toys.

That Sunday, February 14th, to the best of our knowledge, our second son was conceived.

On Monday I reported for work. That was the day classes began at U.C. Riverside for the very first time. I took some photos but had to have them developed at a downtown commercial studio. It would be a few more days before I could convert an old upstairs cleaning closet into a darkroom. Right behind the lead melting pot, it was hot and smelly and about as far from state of the art as one can imagine. But I managed. Within the year we would move into our new building and a darkroom I designed.

Although my salary was only ninety-five dollars a week, I made a deal with Mr. Hays—everybody called him Tim—which allowed me to freelance for magazines. I also got it in writing that I owned my negatives after the paper had published them.

There was, however, another fairly lucrative source for extra cash.

The Press-Enterprise Company published two papers from the same offices, the afternoon Riverside Press and the morning Riverside Enterprise, which circulated mostly in the county. After I worked my eight-hour shift for the afternoon paper, I would take pictures for the Enterprise. They paid three dollars for each picture used. That doesn't sound like much but it added up. Some weeks that amounted to thirty bucks or more.

The organization's legendary thrift policies—some might use the term cheapskates—was best personified by our paymaster, a gnome of a man known as Chappy. We were paid in cash, and it was Chappy who handed out pay envelopes every Friday.

If a reporter wanted a new pencil he first had to show the old pencil stub. Notebooks had to be filled to the last page. Overtime pay was rare and had to be approved ahead of time except in my case.

As the first and only staff photographer I could not avoid it. Salaries were barely competitive, which made my situation unique. With my overtime and extra pay for Enterprise photos I was making more than the city editors.

After a couple of years, one of the editors' wives got pissed.

"Why should Fred get paid more than you," she nagged him, "you work just as hard, if not harder. They can afford to go on vacations we can't."

The result was that I got promoted out of overtime and put on salary. Now I was chief photographer of a one-man department. That stunt cost me close to a thousand bucks. But I had a title. I was the photo editor. It said so on my business cards.

It wasn't too long before I could hire some help. My first was Joe Kennedy, a kid still in high school who worked for me part-time. Joe was a very gifted photographer, who became a star performer for the Los Angeles Times. Many of my later hires became successful photojournalists with metropolitan dailies or national magazines.

My own first so-called scoop came in 1956 when two commercial airliners collided over the Grand Canyon, killing 128 persons. Thanks to a great working relationship with nearby March Air Force Base, I was the only civilian photographer allowed to fly aboard an Air Force SA-16 rescue plane. We got there too late for photos, so I spent the night in a sleeping bag atop one of the wings. Next morning we flew within 200 yards of the wreckage. There wasn't much left to shoot, so no prize-winning photos, but I got there first and a story about yours truly ran in the National Press Photographer magazine.

Prizes did come my way later. My first award was a third-place for features in an Associated Press photo contest. It paid twenty-five dollars. Tim Hays called me into his office to congratulate me and handed me a bonus check for fifty dollars. It was the paper's first editorial department award ever.

The following year I garnered a second place in spot news and two honorable mentions. Again I got called into Tim's office. He commended me for my efforts and handed me a check for twenty-five dollars. I won again the next year, this time a first prize. I am still waiting to hear from Mr. Hays.

The awards kept coming as certificates or plaques, and I duly framed and hung each on the walls of my office. Apparently it was not the right thing to do. When my bragging rights wall hangings reached two dozen, one of my staffers told me quite frankly that such display was ostentatious.

"Look boss," he said by way of explanation, "we know you're good, people know you're good, no need for you to keep reminding us."

He was right of course. I took them all down and stored them in a closet, never to be displayed again.

20

By now I had an agent in New York to handle freelancing. Since Hollywood was within our range of coverage, I took many celebrity photos which Frank Gilloon, my agent, could peddle easily to various fan magazines. Sometimes the way these pictures were being used was simply outrageous.

One particular take of Vince Edwards of TV's Ben Casey fame, and his girlfriend, which I shot with a telephoto lens at Santa Anita race track, was bought by four different fan publications, each of which lied about the details.

One had them fly off to Mexico to get married—they printed a gratuitous picture of a jet flying away—another had them reconcile after a split, yet another said they were on a secret honeymoon. You get the idea, none of it was true. It sold copies and that was all that mattered. My agent's commission was fifty percent, but I still made good money from the many sales.

To tell when you had really arrived in the business back then was to get published in LIFE Magazine. That was the Valhalla of photojournalism. I had had my chance with the Texas dustbowl of 1952, but my pictures were not used. In the early '60s I was still trying. As it turned out my first was a last. Actually a last was my first.

In 1961 the Kingston trio, a hugely popular singing group, gave a concert in San Bernardino, at the Orange Shows Swing Auditorium. It was something we covered as a matter of routine. Backstage to take pictures, I asked the group to pose for a neat threesome. One member of the trio, Dave Guard, refused to pose with the other two, Bob Shane and Nick Reynolds. He insisted I take his picture separately. He was living up to his nickname, Lonesome Dave, but I soon discovered the real reason.

The group was splitting up. This concert was the last time the original Kingston trio would perform. This was Show-biz news, Big-time! And I had the photos.

Early next morning I called my agent, who had already heard about the split.

"I think you are the only photographer to get separate shots of the three," he said. "Get them to me as fast as possible, I'm sure LIFE wants them."

Past experience had taught me not to have my hopes too high. But this time everything worked just right. I air-expressed the negatives to New York, where a messenger picked them up and delivered them directly to the magazine. They got there before deadline, and two postage-stamp sized photos ran side by side in the back of the book.

A last for the Kingston Trio was a first for me in LIFE Magazine. I finally had the prestige of being published in the most respected photography magazine in the country. As for the money, that's a different story.

Since the photos ran really small, LIFE only paid a minimum $25 each. Gilloon's share was fifty percent. Air expressing cost me close to ten bucks. Long distance phone calls added to my cost. I also bought several magazines to send to friends and relatives. All in all I was lucky to break even.

Three years later I shot a first at the same venue.

In 1964 The Rolling Stones gave their first ever American concert in the self same Swing Auditorium. Again I was the lone photographer on the scene, and my picture showed them getting off a bus, with Mick Jagger standing somewhat demurely behind Bill Wyman, as Keith Richards signs autographs out in front.

That picture my agent could not sell.

"Everybody wants pictures of the Beatles," he told me, "they think the Stones are simply too dirty and uncouth.

He may have been close to the truth. According to a famous quote by Tom Wolfe: "The Beatles want to hold your hand, the Rolling Stones want to burn down your town."

After Frank Gilloon died, and his agency was taken over, someone discovered that Stones photo, and immediately sold it for use in a coffee table book on the famous quintet. But that was twenty years later.

When I first established the Press-Enterprise photo department, I devised a filing system for our negatives. I had special envelopes printed, listing subject matter, date, and photographer. The envelopes fit into special cardboard boxes, each a month's worth, stored in filing cabinets.

After a few years we ran out of filing space in the photo lab. I was determined never to throw away a negative. The need very often arose for file photos to illustrate stories. We packed the negative boxes into larger boxes and our head custodian, Al Recio, helped me carry them off to a small attic above the executive rest room.

Al was a good guy. We often played poker together. He would be there when we needed him, be it to fix a stopped up drain, repair a sticky lock, install new fluorescent lights, what have you, Al was the man you called.

Al Recio died of a massive heart attack in 1965 before his 56th birthday. Had he not died I would have killed him.

In keeping with Press-Enterprise fiscal policy, which was to save money wherever possible, Al Recio took it upon himself to sell every negative stored in the attic for silver reclamation. I believe that the company buying the negs paid the paper forty-three dollars, for which the publisher thanked his head custodian.

For my department it represented a disaster. Ten years of work never again available for publication, ten years of archival treasures shot to hell. There was one small consolation. Every so often I would take a negative which I deemed of special importance, and file it in a special place. That certainly proved prescient.

During an appearance at the National Orange Show some time prior to 1965, comedian George Gobel judged a pie-baking contest. The winner was an eleven-year-old boy. As a gag photo to illustrate the event I posed the young man, holding the pie high on one hand, pretending to shove it into Gobel's face. It was a cute photo and got good play.

Five years later we covered a murder case in Riverside, involving an elderly couple who were bound and stabbed to death in their bed. When the police arrested three teen-agers as the murder suspects, one of the names sounded familiar. It turned out to be the same innocent faced pie baker I had photographed with George Gobel. That was a negative I had saved in my personal file.

Another lucky save was a set of photos I had taken of the Good Friday, 1964, earthquake in Alaska. Once more my connections with the Air Force at March AFB helped get me aboard a rescue aircraft. To date that is still the most destructive natural disaster I have ever covered. Southern California being an earthquake prone area, such major catastrophes hold a special interest for our readers.

But those two were isolated incidents. Most of the time, when an editor asked me if I had file photos of a certain event, if it was before 1965, I regretfully had to say no.

"But look at the bright side," I would tell them, dripping with sarcasm, "the paper got forty-three dollars for all that silver."

21

By 1964 our little family had grown. In addition to Guy, our oldest, born in 1952 and David, born in 1954, we had Marc, who came along after a four-year break, in 1958. Actually Vivian did get pregnant in between but had a miscarriage in 1956. The fetus was not far enough along to determine gender, but I'm willing to bet it would have been another boy.

It has never ceased to amaze me how three individuals with identical genetic makeup, raised in identical environment, could turn out so different. Although all three had great creative talents, they chose vastly different fields. Guy became an art historian, eventually becoming a curator at New York's Metropolitan Museum, David followed in my footsteps and became a successful photo journalist, and Marc went into the performing arts, first as an actor and then a drama teacher.

How each got there is a different story. I don't mean to take anything away from David or Marc, both of whom are exceedingly gifted and intelligent individuals, but I believe we would all agree that Guy was the brainiest of the bunch. He got that from his mother. I have always been in awe of Vivian's super intellect, her common sense approach to life, her sensitivity and compassion toward others. I could never match any of those qualities.

Guy excelled in high school, became an A.S.F. student in Holland, was awarded Phi Beta Kappa honors at the University of California and received a scholarship from Princeton.

He was smart from the day he was born. One time, when Guy was two, Vivian took him grocery shopping to the supermarket. Guy began to act up. Vivian tried to rein him in, but he wouldn't stop. Exasperated, she grabbed his arm and said in a stern tone: "Guy, you're acting like a two-year-old!" Back came the answer in a flash: "But mom, I am a two-year-old."

David had a little bit of a rough time getting through high school. Once his talents as a photographer became known—I bought him his first camera when he was eight—the school Yearbook adviser had him take pictures at times during his senior year when he should have been in class, or studying. It was only through the kind intervention of his English teacher, a lady who practically dragged him through finals, that he managed to graduate.

In Junior College, I like to tell my friends, David majored in Choir and Bowling. And yet, once he became a professional news photographer, and a prize-winning one at that, he made more money than either one of his brothers. I think I gave him a pretty good start.

At age ten, as a lark, I got him his own press credential when I took him along on an assignment to cover a visit by Prince Philip of England.

An international press corps waited at the Palm Springs Airport for the arrival of the Prince's plane. The red carpet was rolled out, crowds pressed up against the ropes on either side, press photographers jockeyed for position, and dignitaries waited on the carpet to greet their royal guest.

The Prince arrived, climbed down the steps from his jet, and began his slow walk along the red ribbon of honor, smiling at the crowd and waving. Suddenly there was a small commotion a few feet from where I was pressing against the ropes.

Half the size of everyone else there, David, who couldn't see anything, had crawled through the legs of the people in front of him, exiting on the red carpet inside the ropes. There he sat, camera aimed at the Prince, busy snapping pictures. Taking it all in stride, Prince Philip patted David on the head and said for everyone to hear:

"I say, they're making them rather young here, wouldn't you think?"

Marc was yet another story. In addition to excelling in every sport he tried out for, from the time he was two, you could tell Marc was a performer. He might play at being a cowboy in the morning, a locomotive engineer in the afternoon and a rock musician at night, and each role required the appropriate costume. The constant wardrobe changes kept his mother busy.

Marc performed in just about every high school production, and after graduation went to Cal State Fullerton where he began to study mime. It was a choice that had unforeseen consequences. When the great Marcel Marceau taught a mime workshop at the University of Michigan, Marc enrolled.

At the end of the workshop Marc was hooked. When he came home he informed his mother and me that Marceau had invited him to study in Paris. At first it sounded like a pipe dream.

"Oh sure," I scoffed when he gave us the news, "did he say that to you or did he mime it?"

"No, really dad, he told me I was one of the most gifted students he had ever seen."

"You want to go to Paris? Where you gonna stay, on top of the Eifel Tower?"

"You can ask him yourself, dad, he's performing at Cerritos College a week from Saturday. I told him you might come to talk to him. He said a ticket would be waiting for you at the box office."

Call me a Yiddishe Papa, call me a pushover, I went to Cerritos and met with Marceau.

"Marc tells me you have invited him to study with you in Paris," I said.

"Mais oui, I 'ave indeed. Marc is a very gifted young man."

"Well, Monsieur Marceau, who is going to pay for that?"

"You are, Monsieur Bauman. The world of mime will lose a great talent if you don't."

Well there it was. Fateful words from the mouth of a mime. How could I refuse?

A year later I was on a jet with Marc, bound for Paris. The real estate agent for Marc's small apartment on the Left Bank insisted on being paid in advance for the entire year. Luckily, at Vivian's urging, I had recently acquired an American

Express Gold card. I withdrew four thousand dollars, then hurriedly called my wife in California so she would transfer that amount from Savings.

Marc settled into his apartment in Paris and began to study with Marceau He was there for three years. Vivian and I had agreed to pay for his entire stay. That was made possible only because Vivian had decided to go back to school once our youngest was old enough.

She got her teaching credential from the University of California and later her Master's in Education from the University of Redlands.

Marc was one of only three Americans at that time to earn a diploma from L'Ecole Internationale de Mimodrame de Paris.

Since those years he has directed theatre productions, acted professionally, and taught acting and movement, for over twenty years. He served as artist-in-residence nation-wide, and has taught and directed for top ranked schools throughout the United States and in Europe.

There was one other huge difference between the boys. Guy was gay.

He was eighteen when he told us about it. We had occasionally wondered about his sexual orientation, but there were no outward signs. He was one of the most sensitive human beings I have ever known, but then, lots of straights are sensitive. He dressed conservatively, his manner of speech was forthright and masculine and he dated girls. I sound as though I am stereotyping gays, but I really am not. I am simply stating facts, which helped keep us unaware.

Many gays at that time were still in the closet. Gays were discriminated against broadly and Guy chose to keep his sexual orientation to himself. Once he opened up to us we did everything to show support. It was the natural thing for us to do. We loved him no less and we told him so. We raised our kids to be individuals and they lived up to our expectations.

"Guy, sweetheart," Vivian told him, "all we want for you is to be happy. You live your life the way you feel. There is no shame to that. If I do have one regret it is that you won't have children."

We knew enough about homosexuality to realize that individuals don't chose their lifestyle, they are born to it. For as long as he lived, Guy was Vivian's best friend. Many were the days when they'd talk on the phone for hours.

I am a little ashamed to admit that my reaction initially was that of sorrow. I cried privately but tried to keep up a good front. When I suggested Guy see a psychiatrist, he agreed, probably just to humor me.

"I know you are not going to change, Guy," I explained, "I want you to see an expert in the field to make you feel good about yourself. He should help you to be proud of who you are."

"I hope you are proud of who I am, dad," Guy said pointedly.

"You know I am Guy, I love you."

AIDS was still very much of an unknown disease in the 1970s, but when testing for HIV became almost mandatory for gays in the 1980s, Guy tested positive.

In 1989 Vivian's mother died after a prolonged illness. We had put her into a nursing home in Riverside so that Vivian could see her almost every day.

In 1989 we suffered a disastrous fire that burned down half our home, most of our personal belongings and all of our clothes.

In 1989, while we were living in a hotel following the fire, I got a phone call from Guy in New York that began with him singing a few bars of 'Is That All There Is', Peggy Lee's famous musical lament. He was referring to his grandmother's death and our fire.

"Remember that song, dad?" he asked. "Well that's not all there is. I discovered my first Kaposis Sarcoma today."

We both knew that was a death sentence.

It took me three days to sum up the courage to tell his mother.

I visited Guy in New York for the last time a year later, as he was lying in a rented hospital bed in his small apartment, incontinent and in diapers. His companion Duncan, a charming young man, whom we considered our fourth son, was cleaning him off and changing the diapers, when I made some stupid kind of joke about the situation. I was trying to put on a cheerful face.

"Dad," Guy said reprovingly, "here I am dying, and you are making stupid jokes."

"If I weren't joking I'd be crying, Guy," I tried to justify myself.

"Dad, I want you to cry."

I leaned over to hug him and sobbed uncontrollably for several minutes. It was the last time I saw him alive. Guy died three days later. He was only thirty-eight.

In 1992, the Metropolitan Museum dedicated the entire Volume 27 of its Journal to the memory of Guy Bauman, their associate curator of European Paintings. In the world of art historians, his name lives on.

22

Riverside is halfway between Los Angeles and Palm Springs. The paper reaches out in both directions, covering, besides local news, such things as politics, major league sports to the west and celebrities vacationing in the desert to the east.

When Bing Crosby was newly married to his second wife Cathy, he competed in the Bob Hope Desert Classic golf tournament in Rancho Mirage. Not only was der Bingle grist for the fan mags, his trophy wife, who rode with him in his golf cart, was doubly so. I let a couple of my staffers, probably more competent than me, take care of the golf coverage, while I went after the famous crooner.

He wanted none of it, feeling I was intruding on his private life. While photographers are barred from the fairways so as not to interfere with the players, I dogged the Crosbys between holes, pointing my telephoto lens in their direction at every opportunity. Finally Crosby had enough. He jumped out of his cart, brandishing a putter, yelling at me to leave them alone.

"I'm sorry, Mr. Crosby," I said, "I'm just doing my job. Look sir, all I want is a couple of good shots of you and Cathy in the golf cart. I promise to leave you alone after that."

"You really mean that, son?"

"Yes sir, just a couple of quick shots."

After getting prominent display in our paper, those two photos ran in LOOK magazine. That was almost as good as LIFE.

Celebrities were not the only ones to covet Palm Springs as a getaway spot, so were Presidents of the United States. Of the seven presidents I covered, from Eisenhower to Reagan, only Jimmy Carter and Lyndon Johnson did not vacation there. Eisenhower and Ford established retirement homes in the desert.

President John F. Kennedy loved Palm Springs. Frank Sinatra built a special addition to his house just so that Kennedy could stay there. The President's advisers did not think that such a good idea because of Sinatra's mob connections, so JFK stayed at Crosby's house instead. When Frank Sinatra found out he was being snubbed, he got so furious he tore down the addition.

Somehow a local photographer got pictures of Angie Dickinson in a bikini, while she was sunning herself by Bing Crosby's swimming pool the day Kennedy was due to arrive.

This photographer came rushing into the pressroom of the hotel where the White House press corps was staying, looking for takers.

"Who wants to buy exclusive pix of Angie Dickinson getting ready for the President?" he asked, holding up his camera, "Got em right here."

Two members of the national press contingent grabbed the man by the arms and pinned him up against a wall.

"You ain't got nothing," one of them growled, as they took away his camera, opened it up and exposed the entire roll to light. "You try a stunt like that again and well break your Nikon over your head."

Back then, reporters and photographer covering the President on a regular basis were fiercely protective of him. Those days are long gone.

The last time JFK visited Palm Springs was in the fall of 1963. I got a particularly flattering photo of him walking toward Air Force One. Boyish looking, he was wearing sunshades, smiling broadly, his hair meticulously styled, trailed by a member of the Secret Service. We ran the photo three columns wide on the front page.

A week later I got a phone call from the White House.

"My name is Jerry Behn," the caller told me, "I am the head of the White House Secret Service detail. You took a great photo of the President in Palm Springs last week. That's me right behind him. I wonder if you would send me a copy. I'd be glad to pay you for it."

"I have a better idea, sir. How about I send you two copies, and you have the President autograph one for me? No charge!"

"I'll be happy to do that. I really do think that is one of the best photographs ever taken of the President."

"You flatter me, Mr. Behn, thank you. I'll be looking forward to the picture."

Toward the end October I received a large envelope from the White House with my autographed copy of the presidential photo. On it he had written 'To Fred Bauman with warm regards, John F. Kennedy.'

Unfortunately I did not save the envelope with the date stamp. That may have been one of the last photographs personally autographed by this President.

On November 23rd, John F. Kennedy was assassinated in Dallas, my wife's hometown.

No one could have foretold that his brother Robert Kennedy would also die at the hands of an assassin. I traveled with Bobby on his campaign plane, photographing him seated in front of a home made campaign banner that read 'All the way with RFK'.

Robert Kennedy's last stop, the night before checking into the Ambassador Hotel, was Riverside. Here he campaigned from the top of a flatbed truck outside the Mission Inn to a jam-packed crowd of thousands. I have a nighttime photo of the candidate, back-lit, shirtsleeves rolled up, forearm raised and fist clenched, exhorting the crowd to vote Democratic.

That night I left the campaign, figuring I had enough art to illustrate our story, especially the stuff shot in Riverside. Had I gone on to Los Angeles, who knows where I would have been when Sirhan Sirhan fired the fatal shots. Among the crush of supporters, campaign workers and other photographers, I might have been nowhere near the candidate. On the other hand I might have been close enough to catch a stray bullet.

I met the third Kennedy brother Teddy through John V. Tunney, son of famous boxer Gene, when Tunney began his congressional campaign.

John and Teddy had been roommates at college, and John called on him for political support. Tunney spent time in the Air Force at March Air Force Base, serving with the Attorney General's office.

Upon leaving the service Tunney rented a small house in a working class neighborhood of Riverside as his official residence so he could run for Congress from the district. Teddy Kennedy flew in by helicopter, landing in a vacant field close-by, causing quite a stir in this otherwise Republican bailiwick. I was able to get some great shots of Teddy.

Portraits I took of the three Kennedy brothers are proudly displayed on my den wall. As I sit typing this on my computer, I look up at the picture, and sadly contemplate what might have been.

The Tunney campaign got a real boost the day in 1964 when President Lyndon Johnson came to Riverside. Johnson himself was running for a full term as president, having succeeded to the office after the JFK assassination.

A fellow photographer, Bob Ringquist, who had been with me the longest, and I, persuaded the paper to let us publish a souvenir booklet of the occasion and split the profits. The cover, obviously, was a picture of Johnson addressing the multitude from the steps of the Riverside courthouse. Inside were great photos of Tunney with the President. The booklet sold for a dollar.

To use as something he could autograph for campaign contributors, Tunney asked me if I could print a special edition of the booklet, featuring him on the cover. He ordered five hundred copies.

When I delivered the booklets to his house I got a taste of what real campaign financing comes down to. As California pol Jesse Unruh famously said, "Money is the mother's milk of politics."

Tunney took me to a bedroom, where he hauled a shoebox from a closet shelf. It was stuffed with hundred dollar bills.

"Here you are," he said, counting out five, "that should do it. I'll let you know if I need more."

I am almost positive none of that cash was ever reported.

After three terms in office as congressman, Tunney ran for the U.S. Senate from California. Our executive editor and my boss, Norman Cherniss, a friend of Tunney's, allowed me to take off two months during the fall to become official campaign photographer.

Cherniss, a brilliant newspaperman, who had made the Press-Enterprise a nationally recognized publication—we won a Pullitzer under his leadership—was an ardent Democrat, who would do his best to get the man elected.

It was a somewhat unusual arrangement, since the paper made up the difference between what the campaign could afford to pay me and my regular salary. Cherniss looked upon Tunney as a hometown boy.

The campaign was always short of money. One time in San Francisco we stayed at the Clift Hotel, owned by a friend of the Tunneys. On checking out, there was not enough money to pay the bill. Everyone's credit card was maxed out. Friendship only went so far. The lady owning the hotel wanted to get paid. Somewhat embarrassed, Tunney took me aside.

"Look, Fred," he confided, "we are temporarily flat broke. Would you have an American Express card we can charge the hotel to? I will pay you back as soon as we get home."

My card was good and so was his word.

I have often wondered what would have happened to the Tunney senatorial campaign, had I not pitched in. I got paid back before my next month's American Express bill came due. Tunney won the election and I returned to my regular job.

23

Being near a major Air Force Base and having a good working relationship had its advantages. Apart from the time I was able to fly the rescue mission on the Grand Canyon midair collision story, I took several memorable flights courtesy of the U.S.A.F.

When Alaska was hit by a major earthquake on Good Friday of 1964, I was invited to fly along with a March AFB based rescue plane. It was the largest earthquake ever to hit North America, variously reported as measuring from 8.4 to 9.2 on the Richter Scale. The initial shock waves lasting over five minutes ripped apart streets and buildings, resulting in a death toll of 131, including those from tsunamis in Alaska, California and Oregon.

I shot hundreds of pictures and flew back commercially the next day, enabling the Press-Enterprise to publish exclusive photos by one of their own staffers, a feat not matched by many other papers our size.

As it turned out we almost didn't make it. On the flight up there, our SA-16 Albatross Search and Rescue plane, a bone-rattling propeller driven Grumman production, experienced a cabin fire of electrical origin. Like everybody else on board, I was dressed in a flight suit with a parachute strapped to my back. As an alarm signal went off, Sgt. Walters, the crew chief told me to get up from my bucket seat. He stepped behind me and cinched tight the straps between my legs, pinching the family jewels to a point where it almost hurt.

"You may have to use this, sir," he said, "just making sure the straps don't snap hard when the chute opens. Might break some bones, sir!"

A wisp of smoke was curling up from a control panel just above the navigator.

"What are you talking?" I asked nervously, sucking in my breath. "We may have to bail out!? Jesus Christ, we're over Puget Sound. If the fall don't kill me I'm certainly going to drown. No way buddy!"

"If we do, you go first," Sergeant Walters insisted. "As the only civilian on board, your safety is my responsibility. You're first, even if I have to shove you out, sir."

I conjured up visions of my standing in the plane's open doorway, desperately grabbing hold of anything I could to hang on, while the crew chief was standing behind me, one foot firmly planted in the small of my back, trying to loosen my grip to kick me out.

Actually it took less than forty seconds to contain the fire and put it out, but it seemed like an eternity. Apparently the damage wasn't such that we had to make an emergency landing at the closest air base.

We continued our flight north and with my legs a little unsteady, I made my way up to the navigator to pat him on the back.

"Nice work there," I complimented him, "for a few seconds you had me worried."

"Little problems like that are almost par for the course with this old bird," he explained. "After a while you get used to them. Never had to bail out yet."

It may have been a small problem for him, but I don't ever want to live through another one like that myself.

The Good Friday earthquake was not the first time I flew to Alaska with the Air Force.

In 1959, with the Cold War at its chilliest, I accompanied a March AFB bomber crew to Eielson AFB in Alaska where they had been assigned temporary duty at an alert facility. This was an area apart from the rest of the base where crews lived, ate and slept 24/7 in case they were called upon to fly at a moment's notice, ready to drop atomic bombs on an enemy.

To this day the official line of the government has been never to admit or deny that nuclear weapons were being stored then at places like the huge concrete and earthen storage bunkers about a half-mile west of the freeway that runs alongside March AFB. This despite the fact that I had actually taken a photo of a tarp covered bomb being transported from there to the base on an Air Force flatbed truck. I also watched the loading of one aboard a B-47 bomber, although no photographs were permitted. It was similar in shape and size to the rotating barrel of a cement truck.

The Strategic Air Command flyboy trio on TDY I was assigned to included Capt. Earl Cairl, Capt. Robert Newly, and Lieut. Ralph Langford. They made up the cew of a B-47 bomber, without doubt a nuclear weapon equipped plane.

For days now klaxons had sounded the alarm, sometimes twice a day, which had crews scrambling to their planes ready to take off. SAC was fully prepared to unleash total destruction on any power foolish enough to start a nuclear war. All the alarms had been for practice. The goal of the Command was that the first plane be ready for take off three minutes after the sounding of an alert, the last plane be airborne in fifteen minutes.

On this day word had thankfully come down from headquarters that there would be no more practice alerts. "The next klaxon you hear will be the real thing," the men had been told.

These instructions were in effect as Capt. Cairl and his crew stood on the flight line by their plane, engaged in pre-flight checks before a training flight, waiting for the ground crew to show up. Suddenly over the hubbub of preparations came the sound of the klaxons. The men stared at each other, each wondering if the others had heard. Of course they had. That jarring noise was unmistakable.

Then the ground maintenance crew came roaring up in their weapons carrier as they had done for practice so many times before.

"That was the klaxon all right," the crew chief yelled, "this is the real thing!"

Had the Russians attacked? Were there missiles on the way? Had the United States opted for a pre-emptive strike? At this point anything was a possibility, but nothing these men had not trained for long and hard.

I described what followed in an article I wrote for PARADE Magazine at the time.

Capt. Cairl stood as if transfixed for a full three seconds—an instant to be sure—but to him it seemed like an eternity. Then he jumped up the plane's ladder as if jabbed by en electric prod and scrambled into the cockpit. "Let's get this mother out of here!" he yelled.

Lt. Langford's hands were shaking. It took him a while to get started on his routine navigation procedures which eventually would lead to the arming of the plane's nuclear device.

Capt. Neely was the one member of the crew who took matters in stride. He had had previous combat experience, and his only thought as he began going through the abbreviated check list required of the co-pilot during an alert was "We'll be the first American plane to get shot at this time!"

The B-47 began taxiing down the runway, four of its six jet engines warming to full throttle when the message crackled over the radio.

"Abort, repeat, abort! Disregard…disregard…this is a practice alert!"

The plane was still some distance from getting airborne. There was little trouble shutting down the engines and returning to the alert facility. Capts. Cairl and Neely slumped back in their seats. Up front in the navigator's hole Lt. Langford fought nausea. Nobody said a word. Then they all began talking at once, mouthing several choice epithets into their mikes.

"All of a sudden I felt boiling mad," Lt. Langford said later. "After all that was some shock on the nervous system. They—Cairl and Neely—have had combat experience. I have not. I was shook up, but then my training took over."

Capt. Cairl detailed some of the feelings men like him have when they go on TDY to a base like Eielson.

"You sort of shift into neutral when you go up there," he said. "You really can't have many feelings or you'd go crazy just waiting. I guess my wife will kill me when she reads this, but one doesn't even think much about your family, especially when you are flying. It takes up all your brain processes just to go about your piloting duties."

Capt. Neely also shared his views on the subject of alerts:

"It's just a job, like somebody in a grocery store. Somebody has to do it, and believe me I'd rather be there making history, than at home reading about it. But don't think it is ever routine."

That was almost fifty years ago. I had a tough time getting the Air Force to agree to the PARADE article, especially the part of how the crew reacted to the false alert. Lt. Langford actually spewed his guts out onto the tarmac, but I agreed to leave that part out of the story.

Flying with the Air Force was always fun though sometimes quite challenging. Once on assignment during a mid-air refueling mission I reached a little beyond my capabilities.

We were flying KC-97 tankers, those air-borne gas stations that gave fighters and bombers unlimited range, regardless of which part of the globe they were operating in. Refueling in mid air takes an enormous amount of skill.

The boom operator lies flat on his stomach in the rear of the plane, guiding a nozzle from his craft into a receptacle on the trailing plane flying slightly below him, but at precisely the same speed. He is in constant radio communication with both his own pilot, and that of the aircraft being refueled. It takes steady nerves and good eyesight.

Photographing the scene, I too was flat on my stomach, above but to the side of the boom operator. I don't know who felt more stress. Upon successful completion of the training mission I needed to relax.

Strolling up into the cockpit I casually mentioned to the co-pilot that I might want to try flying this baby. I had flown Piper Cubs and single-engine Cessnas on aerial photo shoots though never without the real pilot aboard.

"You want to give it a go?" I was asked. I was not about to chicken out. The pilot had vacated his seat to get a drink or something and I settled in behind the controls.

"We are flying on auto-pilot, are we not? I asked. This was some fun pretence and I was having a ball. The co-pilot had put the earphones on my head.

"We are right now, but I'll switch it off if you want me to. Just go easy on the controls. These crates practically fly themselves. Keep your eye on the artificial horizon and the altimeter."

I was too stubborn to say no. With sweaty palms I was holding grimly on to the wheel, apparently without realizing that I was over reacting and pulling back on the controls much too hard. Our plane was rapidly gaining altitude.

We were flying in formation with three other tankers. Suddenly a message came crackling over the radio. It was from the plane behind us:

"Who the hell is flying that ship!?" the message asked.

"Oh we got some civilian reporter with us," the co-pilot radioed back. "He thinks he can fly!"

"Well tell him he can't do an Immelman (loop) in a KC-97."

That was my last attempt ever to try something I didn't know beans about. When we returned to base, the story had preceded us. I was the object of much affectionate kidding in the Officers Mess. It cost me quite a few rounds.

24

With newspaper headlines, as with TV coverage, bad news always trumps good news. The greater the disaster, the bigger the headline.

At the Press-Enterprise we had a city editor, Jim Hushaw, who was famous for one thing. When photographers went on an accident and announced their arrival at the scene, the first words out of his mouth over the two-way radio were: "How many dead?"

When I was a cub reporter at the Denison Herald, covering the police beat, one of my duties was to make a series of phone calls shortly before deadline. The numbers were those in outlying areas of Sheriff substations, volunteer fire departments, funeral parlors or just local tipsters, who fancied them selves reporters, and whom we paid a few dollars to keep an eye on their community.

Most of the time I didn't even know who I was calling, it was all just part of the routine. Here is how one phone call went:

Me: "Hi, this is Bauman at the Herald. Anything happen we should know about?"

Him: "Matter of fact there is. We had a fatal head-on about a half hour ago, out U.S. 82, near Bells."

Me: "Fatal you say? Good, I hope they're all dead."

The moment those words crossed my lips I regretted having said that. I began to apologize profusely.

Me: "Gosh I'm sorry, I really am. I should never have said that. You must think I'm totally insensitive, but please let me explain, we're on deadline, and you know, four dead makes a bigger headline than one or two dead."

I rambled on only to have him interrupt me.

Him: "Gee, I hope they're all dead too, I'm the local undertaker!"

I had found a kindred spirit. I guess it all depends on whose perspective you are coming from.

In this business you have to develop a tough gut. I hated covering accidents involving children, but it is all part of the job, and I wouldn't let anyone stop me from taking pictures.

A Riverside police captain tried it once.

Not long after we moved into our new building a small child was killed in a traffic accident on a street right next to the paper's parking lot. When I heard the location over the police radio, I grabbed my camera and rushed downstairs. It was a pitiful scene.

The child had pulled away from its mother and rushed into the street. The driver of the car that hit her had no way of spotting the child before it was too late. The tot ran out from between two parked cars. It was definitely not the driver's fault.

The mother was kneeling next to the child's body with her back to me, and Captain Gene Fagan, who had arrived a few seconds before me, was also kneeling down, positioning himself as a shield between me and the victim.

When he saw me raise my camera to record the scene, he pointed a finger at me and snarled: "If you take this picture I'll have you run out of town!"

"You try doing that, captain," I said. "This is a public street, and I have every right to shoot pictures."

The photo I took showed the captain threatening me, with just a portion of the victim's body showing. His gesture made it that much more dramatic. I found out later what motivated him to act the way he did.

The unfortunate driver of the car was the co-owner of a local car agency. It was the car dealership from which the Riverside Police Department bought all their vehicles. I don't know if any kickbacks were involved in those deals but there certainly was a cozy relationship between the two.

I returned to the office to develop and print the picture, then showed it with some pride to the editors.

"That's a great picture, but we're not going to use it," I was told.

"Why the hell not?" I asked, "I think it should make the front page."

"Mr. Hays got a call from Police Chief Bennett, asking him not to use it."

"No shit! Since when do we let the police department censor the news?"

"Get wise, Fred," the news editor told me, "That car dealership is one of our biggest advertisers."

Ordinarily our advertising department did not have any input about what ran or didn't run in the news columns. In this instance, push had come to shove and shove won. It was not that surprising. Mr. Hays, Chief Bennett and the agency's owner all were members of the same downtown Kiwanis Club.

"Can I put the picture on the wire?" I asked.

"Sure, so long as it doesn't run in Riverside."

I put the picture on the UPI wire. As a result almost every Southern California Daily ran a version of it on their front page. When contest time came around, it won first place in the UPI photo contest. My paper announced the win and finally used the photo, way inside and small, almost a year after the event.

Another attempt to stop me from taking pictures occurred when a B-47 bomber on a training mission, crashed and burned near March Air Force Base. You could never be certain whether a plane was carrying a nuclear weapon or not.

The crash occurred off base, about a mile from the runway, killing the entire crew. We got the word as soon as the crash happened from a passing driver with a mobile phone. I arrived at the crash site shortly after base and local fire crews had extinguished the flames, about the same time military police were trying to secure the area. The plane had made large crater. In order to see it I had to climb a small incline.

As I ran toward the crash, I was stopped by a military policeman.

"You can't take any pictures here, sir," he warned, "we've come to secure the area until a press relations officer shows up."

"I'm on public property. I can shoot anything I want to."

It was an unfortunate choice of words.

"Sir, I am authorized to shoot you if you get any closer," he said, pointing a weapon at me.

"Go ahead and shoot! I know my rights."

I suppose such bravado could have got me killed. Instead the airman got flustered about what to do next. He got on his walkie-talkie to call his superior officer. I do not know what he was told. Apparently I got the go-ahead from HQ.

"You can takes pictures, sir," I was told by an obviously frustrated MP, "but then I cannot let you leave until the press relations officer shows up."

"That's fine, thank you, no problem."

Permitting me to take photos at close range told me one thing. There was no atom bomb aboard. When the major from the press office showed up he confirmed that.

"We cannot stop you from taking photos," he said, "what concerns us is that you do not show bodies."

Maybe he could differentiate between what may have been a body and what was other debris. All the victims were so badly charred they blended in with the rest of the crash site.

A few days after the crash, the grieving young widow of one of the pilots showed up at my office. I thought she had come to complain about our use of the photo. What she wanted was a copy. She explained that for her, looking at the scene served as closure.

Even the Secret Service tried to trample on my freedom of the press.

During the height of the Cambodian crisis, when Nixon was secretly bombing that country, Henry Kissinger, architect of that policy was hiding from the news media. One of our Palm Springs reporters traced down a rumor that the Secretary of State was staying at Hollywood producer Bob Evans' house there.

I decided to check it out in person, but before I left Riverside, I called TIME Magazine, knowing they would be very interested in any art I might get of the elusive Dr. Kissinger. I also called because, with their White House contacts, they might be able to facilitate access.

Evans' house was on a cul-de-sac in an exclusive area of Palm Springs. The fence in front of the home was the kind where the slats are set at a slant, so that from a certain angle one could see through it.

I had no difficulty spotting my prey from across the street and began to photograph him through the fence with a telephoto lens. Kissinger rested by the pool, sunning himself, his thong-clad feet facing the camera, baggy swim trunks covering his rotund belly, sunglasses shading his eyes.

After firing off a roll with my motor, I quickly emptied the camera and stuck the film in my pocket. I knew what was about to happen.

A Secret Service guy rushed out of the front door and yelled for me to stop shooting.

"You can't take pictures here," he told me without giving any reason.

"I believe Dr. Kissinger is a public figure and as such fair game for photographers," I countered.

"There is no one here by that name," the agent insisted.

"How about Heinrich Kissinger?" I quipped.

The agent had no sense of humor. "I will have to ask you to give me the film in your camera," he commanded.

"For taking pictures of someone you say is not here?"

"You're shooting a private residence."

"From across the street and on public grounds. If Kissinger is not here, why are you?"

The agent had no answer.

"If I get on my car radio I can have a dozen reporters and photographers here in fifteen minutes. You want that? Why not ask the man to come out for a couple of shots and then I'll leave him alone, ok?"

The agent disappeared into the residence while I waited. I noticed that Kissinger had left the pool area. Some twenty minutes later he appeared, fully clothed, with his host Bob Evans. By this time our reporter had arrived and was busy taking notes. I took a half dozen pictures of the two men and left the scene true to my words.

My newspaper, and many others, used the unflattering poolside photo, which I had put on the UPI wire. TIME used the more flattering shot of Evans and the Secretary of State in front of the residence.

Marty Haymaker, photo coordinator for TIME Magazine's Los Angeles office, told me the next day that the Nixon White House was furious about the coverage.

"When we called them to confirm Kissinger's presence in Palm Springs," Marty told me, "they tried to have me pull you off the assignment. I told them there was no way I could reach you. You're probably on Nixon's 'shit list' now."

"No kidding! Well if I am, that's something to be proud of."

Shooting a photo is one thing. Deciding whether to use it or not is another. I have always told photographers who worked for me that their first duty was to cover the news, no matter what. Their job was not to censor an event, no matter how they felt about it. If one of my staffers had ever come back from an assignment and told me that the scene was simply too gruesome to film I would have fired him or her on the spot.

One of the saddest accident scenes I ever covered involved the traffic death of another toddler. This one happened outside a private child-care facility on a dead-end street. As parents drove up to collect their offspring, one little girl tried to run toward her mother's car. She never made it. Another parent, driving entirely within the speed limit, unknowingly ran over her.

When I arrived on the scene, the dead girl's mother was kneeling on the pavement, arms raised toward heaven, a silent scream on her distorted face, the entire front of her blouse covered in blood. I took my pictures with a semi-telephone lens, far enough away so as not to intrude physically into her private grief.

Returning to the office, I called an editorial meeting myself, wondering whether we should use the photo, and if so, how big and what section of the paper. It was a hard decision all the way around. In the end we did use it on the front of our local section. It was an effort to both shock and warn our readers to be extra careful when driving with children around. In that regard, if the picture served to save just one life, we considered our decision justified.

Many of our readers did not see it that way. The majority wrote that we had unnecessarily intruded on the woman's privacy and should never have published so graphically disturbing an image. Interestingly enough, nobody complained when we published pictures of Somali rebels dragging dead American airmen through the streets. Reader acceptance of such art apparently is in inverse proportion to the distance at which it occurs. In other words, the closer to home, the less we want to see victims of violence.

Nowadays I am glad that I am no longer in the business. With age comes compassion. I have seen my share of tragedy and triumphs. Since my retirement in 1990, other than a couple of trade publication covers, I have not taken a single professional picture. I leave that to my son and his colleagues.

By the way, he did not achieve his position by nepotism. I refused to hire him, but Norman Cherniss, executive editor and my boss, overruled me. Three candidates had applied for the job.

"Can you give me an unbiased opinion of who is best qualified?" Cherniss asked me.

"I don't know if that's entirely possible, but even considering a tiny bias, David stands head and shoulders above the others. But as his father I will not hire him."

"That's okay, I will hire him," Cherniss said. "Tell him if he has any problems with his boss to come see me."

As of this writing, David has celebrated 30 years with the Press-Enterprise. When the second Gulf War started, the paper, now owned by the Belo Corporation of Dallas, sent him as an embedded photographer with the Marines to Iraq.

Thank God he returned safely.

978-0-595-41770-4
0-595-41770-1

www.ingramcontent.com/pod-product-compliance
Lightning Source LLC
Chambersburg PA
CBHW030742180526
45163CB00003B/898